FIRST SERIES

The Collectors Encyclopedia of

ROSEVILLE POTTERY

BY

Sharon and Bob Huxford

COLLECTOR BOOKS

A Division of Schroeder Publishing Co., Inc.

Plate 1: Silver Overlay, 2½", no mark

Additional copies of this book may be ordered from:

COLLECTOR BOOKS
P.O. Box 3009
Paducah, Kentucky 42001
or
The authors: Sharon & Bob Huxford
1202 7th Street
Covington, Indiana 47932

$19.95 plus $1.00 for postage and handling

ISBN: 0-89145-015-7
2nd printing — 1977; 3rd printing — 1979; 4th printing — 1980

Printed by Taylor Publishing Company, Dallas, Texas

This book is dedicated
to
Ed and Thelma,
Marvin and Jan,
and
Roseville collectors
everywhere . . .

"The genius of the artist here calls together the primeval elements beneath his feet, to do his bidding. Earth, water, and fire, bend to the task, and to him bring the product of their united labors. He clothes the varied shapes of beauty in the soft rich colors that please him best. And then across each shinning bossom he lays with exquisite grace a nodding iris . . . a spray of apple blossoms . . . or a rosy thistle bloom . . . And in their fadless triumphant beauties sends them forth to adorn and bless the homes and lives of the children of men . . ."

Lura Milburn Cobb

TABLE OF CONTENTS

ACKNOWLEDGEMENTS

With deepest gratitude we wish to acknowledge the assistance of the many, many, wonderful people who have so generously contributed to this study.

Ed and Thelma Newman have been Roseville collectors for several years and have been our "right arm" over the past several months. At considerable expense, they have added many pieces of pottery to their already extensive collection, so that it would be available to us. Several hundred pieces of fine pottery from their collection were photographed for this book. To these dear friends . . . a special "Thank you."

We're also very grateful to our friends, Marvin and Jeanette Stofft. Their collection contains many fine examples of the Rozane lines of 1905 and 1906 and, because we were so graciously allowed to photograph them . . . as well as several other lines . . . nearly all of the Roseville lines have been well represented. We thank them for this opportunity; and for the hours we spent with them, discussing the pottery and learning from their experience.

Donald and Zeta Alexander have shown us very gracious hospitality on several occasions, and we want to thank them, not only for their encouragement, but also for allowing us to reproduce for our book their own compositions of the Roseville trademarks. Several pieces from their collection are shown in black and white in the picture section.

Buck and Marilyn Jones loaned us several beautiful color slides, which they allowed us to reproduce, for which we thank them very much. Their excellent photography was done by P. L. Hill, Tulsa, Oklahoma.

Other collectors, dealers, and friends who have supplied pottery, or helped in numerous other ways are listed below:

Maxine Fergeson, Wayside Antiques, Zanesville, Ohio.

Betty Blair, Catalpa Heights Antiques, Jackson, O.

Norm and Martha Miller, Schube's Antiques, Franklin, Ind.

Harry and Martha Rheapp

Larry, Linda, and Tony Newman

Virginia Buxton

Bob and Maxine Lang

Thanks to Dana Curtis, our very fine photographer . . . the pictures are just beautiful, Dana!

And lastly, to the staff at the Ohio Historical Society, and especially to Arlene Peterson, Reference Librarian, we send our appreciation.

The progress we were able to make on our research has been almost unbelievable to us. But it has been so only because of these fine people. It was as though they joined with us in a team effort . . . each one striving to do a part to make this study as complete and as accurate as was humanly possible. This has been our goal.

ABOUT THE AUTHORS

The Huxfords are both native Hoosiers and have resided for the past ten years in Covington, a small town on the "banks of the Wabash" near the center of the Indiana state line. They have three children: Marka, 16; Michael, also 16; and Steve, who is 14.

Bob is employed at the Olin Chemical Corporation, and Sharon operates a beauty shop in their home. Both are active members of the Maranatha Baptist Church.

They have been avid collectors with a variety of interests for many years. They are the authors of the book, THE STORY OF FIESTA, and have written several authoritative articles.

Sharon and Bob Huxford

FOREWORD

The art of pottery . . . how and when it all began . . . is an uncertainty whose revelation is obstructed by countless eons and civilizations — obliterating from all but our imagination, glimpses of the ancient cultures. Perhaps women, needing pots for food and water, with an inventiveness born of necessity, noticed how the sun-baked ruts in the clay soil held the water long after a sudden summer shower had passed . . . or a loving father, who days before had fashioned from the pliable, yellow clay a crude horse to entertain his young child, stood and pondered over its brick-like texture.

In such a way, then, as civilizations and cultures progressed and as man aspired to continually improve and improvise . . . so the development of the ceramic art progressed. In the beginning, man shaped these crude vessels of clay by hand . . . perhaps learning to mold bowls around a smooth round rock or by coiling thinly rolled strips to form the sides of cylindrical forms. They left them to harden and bake in the sun. Then, to the previously utilitarian clay-ware, he began to add embellishments and decorations, delighted with the opportunity to satisfy the innate desire man has always possessed, to express with his hands the beauty his senses have revealed to his soul.

As knowledge increased, crude kilns were constructed. Progressing further . . . by some stroke of genius, the potter's wheel was developed, one of man's first mechanical inventions . . . indicating the preeminence of this art in ancient cultures. Its invention was claimed by both the Chinese and the Egyptians.

Sherds of ancient pottery, as well as clay tablets and the painted walls of the tombs, are remarkably preserved. Through their study, modern man has been provided with much understanding of these by-gone civilizations.

Existing evidence indicates an almost simultaneous development in China and Egypt . . . Greek and Roman cultures merged . . . and as the Roman Empire widened with each new conquest, the science of ceramics pervaded the European countries.

The knowledge of pottery that passed on to France and Spain had reached a high degree of proficiency and sophistication. From these peoples, this knowledge advanced to Britain.

The ancient Chinese were responsible for spreading the art to Japan. The inventive Japanese artisans ornamented their pottery with designs in relief by pinching up the still damp clay . . . and adding still more design by incising lines in artistic arrangements.

Although evidences have been found of glazed pottery in ancient Egypt, and at a somewhat later period in Chinese history, nowhere else has ever been found the lustrous glazes of Persia. In this country, the ancient potters learned the use of metallic oxides to produce a glaze that could simulate the platina of metal. After the Arabs conquered Persia, though they had no art of their own, they quickly absorbed the knowledge of the Persian artists. Through the Moors, who were also of the Mohammedan religion, the potters' art was carried on to Africa.

The Sgraffito technique is known to have been used in Italy after the fall of the Roman Empire. Here was developed the first general use of the tin enamel called Majolica. Italian workmen carried the art to France; thus the French were able to produce a ware almost identical. This French tin enameled pottery was called Faience . . . so named after the city of Faenza, the great pottery center.

The art progressed on to Germany where artists and artisans concentrated on the modeling of stoneware — from here came the invention of the salt glaze, which has proven to be very popular with modern day collectors.

Around 1650, Delft pottery became a thriving trade in the Netherlands, and much of the ware was exported. It was characterized by the use of a beautiful blue glaze decorating a white background. Later, as Chinese and Japanese designs were attempted green, red, yellow, and finally black and rose were added.

In England, Staffordshire became the pottery center and from the 18th Century produced novelties such as figurines and Toby jugs. Josiah Wedgwood made a wide variety of artistic, classic stoneware, and the technical processes practiced at his factory contributed valuably to the art.

Long before America was discovered, the Indians were making pottery of simple and original design. The Mound Builders of the Mississippi Basin show evidence of a high degree of culture. The Pueblo dwellers of the Southwest used the coil method, imitating in their pottery the appearance of their woven baskets. Later, their pottery became more graceful, in better proportion, and brightly decorated with color. The Maya Indians were unaware of the potters' wheel, as were the other tribes, even though some of their altar stones were designed on a circular principal. Yet their pottery shows fine symmetry of form. Decorations were incised, stamped or painted on with slip.

After the colonists settled in America, no later than 1650, several potteries in Virginia were turning out crude household wares. In South Carolina, in 1765, a superior clay was discovered and potted there, resulting in such a fine ware that Wedgwood considered it a threat. However, the pottery closed after operating only briefly and left no trace. Other potteries flourished for a short time in New York and Pennsylvania, Philadelphia, Massachusetts and Connecticut. But since there was no popular market with the colonists who preferred the imported English wares, these also soon disappeared.

The first potteries of any permanence were situated in Ohio where there was an abundance of the raw materials necessary to the making of pottery . . . dense clay beds and a plentiful supply of natural gas. Ohio had a growing transportation network that was steadily reaching further beyond its boundaries. Its population was growing, and from its heritage emerged native potters possessing the skill and know-how that resulted from long and diligent dedication to their craft.

In the late 1800's, interest began to grow among the socially prominent young ladies in the delicate art of china painting. As interest continued, the art of ceramic decorating was no longer considered a mere pastime, but had developed into a fledgling art industry.

Scores of potteries sprang up in the immediate vicinity of Zanesville, Ohio, a small town situated on the Muskingum River . . . earning that place the title of "The Clay City"! It was here, in 1891, that the pottery which holds our attention was founded: The Roseville Pottery Co.

THE HISTORY OF ROSEVILLE POTTERY

from beginning to end . . .

George F. Young, upon completion of his education in schools of his native county, entered into the field of education. Although he was held in high regard as a teacher, he left this profession after four years, moving to Zanesville in 1884 where he enrolled in a business college. Completing his course, he accepted the position of bookkeeper with the Singer Manufacturing Company and worked there for 6 years.

When the Roseville Pottery Company was incorporated on January 4, 1892, Young became general manager. Two years prior to this, the company had gone into the production of stoneware, having purchased the facilities of the J. B. Owens Pottery in Roseville, Ohio. With three coal-fired kilns they continued to produce the wares that had been made there by Owens — wares such as flower pots, cuspidors, umbrella stands, and cooking utensils, none of which were marked.

Within a short time, Young had been promoted to Secretary, and, at the close of the first year, was made Secretary and Treasurer. Charles S. Allison was the first President of the Company; J. F. Weaver was Vice President; and Thomas Brown served in the capacity of Treasurer before Young took the office. On the board of directors, in addition to the officers, were: J. L. Pugh of Zanesville and J. N. Owens of Roseville. At the time of organization the capitol stock of the company was $25,000. By 1905, the Muskingum County, Ohio Biography states that the authorized capitol had been increased to $300,000! It was under the continuing leadership and brilliant direction of Young that the Roseville Pottery Company achieved its tremendous success, growing from this single plant employing 45 men in its infancy to a giant of commercial artware whose sales during World War II had reached a staggering $1,250,000. Young eventually became principal stockholder, and four generations of his family followed him in the management of the firm.

In 1898, their market growing and their facilities inadequate, the company expanded, purchasing the plant formerly owned by the Midland Pottery in Roseville; they thereby added three more kilns to the operation. In the same year the company moved their main office to Zanesville, Ohio. Although relocated, the company retained the use of the Roseville name. In Zanesville, they purchased the Clark Stoneware plant on Linden Avenue, formerly used by Peters and Reed. They enlarged and improved the facilities, erecting a three-story building of 50 × 156 feet and installed the latest machinery known to the trade. It was at this location, two years later, that the art pottery was produced.

In 1901, the company acquired the Muskingum Stoneware plant, formerly the Mosaic Tile Company located at Muskingum Avenue and Harrison Streets, in Zanesville. Here their German cookingware was made.

The Company then controlled and operated four plants under the firm title, each with its own superintendent. They were equipped with a total of thirty periodic kilns and provided employment for 325 people.

DEVELOPMENT OF THE ROZANE ART POTTERY

The vogue of ceramic decorating that had begun with such enthusiasm in the latter 1800's had continued, and the interest it stirred was reason enough for several potteries to be established with the intent of capitalizing on the growing interest in art pottery. The Rookwood Pottery of Cincinnati, Ohio, founded in 1880, produced a line of art pottery on a dark blended background, decorated with floral studies executed by hand under the glaze. The line was called Standard. The success of Rookwood attracted and prompted W. A. Long of Steubenville to enter the field with a similar line which he had developed after years of long and dedicated study. His line was called Lonhuda.

In 1893, after seeing the fine exhibits of art pottery on display at the Worlds' Columbian Exposition, S. A. Weller . . . already a successful Zanesville potter of commercial wares . . . realized its potential market. In 1895, he negotiated with Long for the purchase of the Lonhuda Pottery and learned from him his methods of producing Lonhuda. Their association was brief and unpleasant; it was a deluded Long that took his methods and ideas with him to the J. B. Owens Pottery and there instructed artists and technicians in his procedure. Their art line was called Utopian and was, of course, a duplication of Lonhuda. Weller continued the production of Lonhuda, changing the name to Louwelsa, and in a few years had become a wealthy man.

By 1900, Young felt that the Roseville Pottery Company was well enough equipped and staffed to contend with Weller for a share of the profits. He hired Ross Purdy to develop Roseville's first art line. His creation, a duplication of Lonhuda and Louwelsa, was called Rozane — a word coined from the firm's title and location. Rozane was a finely modeled line — ranging from shapes with full rounded bowls and long slender necks ending in deeply flutted rims — to those of simplest classic proportions. Fine artists decorated the dark, blended backgrounds with nature studies, floral sprays, animals, portraits of well-known personalities and American Indians. At the Historical Society in Columbus, Ohio, among the Roseville catalogues and records, is a brochure of art studies which were available for reproduction on the Rozane at the cost of less than 50¢ each. Some are easily recognized Rozane studies. While several smaller pieces might be finished in a day, larger pieces with more detailed painting could require several days. The first Rozane was marked in one of several ways, the most common are ROZANE or RPCO; both die impressed on the bottom of the piece. (See section on Marks for additional
RPCo
information.)

The smaller 5″ — 6″ Rozane ware vases and bowls were offered for sale at prices from $5 to $12; the very large 24″ — 30″ floor vases sold from $50 — $90. For at least one sales promotion, the ware was presented as "Hollywood Ware" — the colored plate in the old catalogues that brought this to our attention bears the circular seal which has a narrow notched band around the circumference and the words Hollywood Ware in script within the circle.

Azurean was a line developed in 1902, similar to Weller's blue Louwelsa. It was a blue and white underglaze decorated art ware on a blue blended background. Some pieces were marked with AZUREAN, die impressed; but often simply RPCO. The lovely Azurean is very scarce today.

In 1904, the Rozane ware trademark was registered with the U. S. Patent Office. Patent # 43,793 was issued to cover its use. The mark that was thereafter used to identify the Rozane art line was a circular ceramic disk or seal with the words ROZANE WARE embossed over the outline of a long stem rose. During the 1907 depression, in an attempt to decrease production expenses, the seal was copied in green ink on a paper sticker. (Donald E. Alexander, Roseville Pottery for Collectors). These were easily removed and no doubt account for many unmarked Rozane ware pieces.

OTHER ART LINES ADDED

While their commercial lines were probably their most profitable, the art lines drew attention to the pottery and gained for them prominence and prestige. In order to keep pace with his Zanesville competitors, Young had to respond to their new art lines with one from the Roseville pottery. As these new art lines were developed, the trade name Rozane became a generalized term used to indicate all art lines. In 1904, the original Rozane line was renamed Rozane Royal. In addition to the dark brown backgrounds, the Rozane Royal "lights", or pastel shades, were introduced. The same technique of underglaze slip painting was executed in soft greys, blues, greens, ivory, and rose shades. The line was marked with the Rozane ware ceramic seal with the particular line name, Royal, in block letters, enclosed in an attached arc below. Several other art lines bore this type of seal. (See section on Marks.)

Rozane Egypto was an art line added in 1904. Christian Neilson, a native of Denmark and a graduate of the Royal Academy of Art at Copenhagen, was its creator. Egypto featured a matte glaze in a soft shade of old green and was modeled in low relief after examples of ancient Egyptian pottery.

Capturing 1st prize at the St. Louis Expedition in 1904, Roseville's Rozane Mongol . . . a high gloss oxblood red line . . . gained recognition for the company and for its creator, John J. Herold. Herold, a native of Austria who was superintendent of the art department from 1900-1908, formulated the copper glaze after the fashion of the Chinese Sang de Boeuf, which was already considered a lost art at the time of the Chia Ching reign of the 16th century. Mongol shapes were typical of Chinese vase forms. Although it represented an important contribution to the field of art pottery, Mongol was not popular with the general public, and quite probably the Company lost money on its production.

Occasionally a shape bearing the Rozane Mongol seal has been found in a blue or green high gloss glaze. In the picture section of this book you will see such a piece as this in a buff color. Roseville authorities term these colors experimental and point out that the artists and technicians were always encouraged to experiment. In the BOOK OF POTTERY AND PORCELAIN (Warren Cox, Crown Publishers, Inc., 1970, Vol 1, p. 556.) we found a very interesting and enlightening theory discussed — one that may have been familiar to early Roseville artisans, perhaps to Herold himself. The text contains these words concerning the glazes and color of fine examples of K'ang Hsi Sang de Beoufs:

> The inside of most specimens is finished with a buff crackled glaze . . . and in fact, specimens are found which are covered all over with this light glaze. Very often the red glaze slips down irregularly . . . leaving . . . buff areas . . . the red could only be brought out in the impurities existing in a muffle kiln. He states that he could turn the reddest piece blue or green by refiring in a kiln that would drive off the impurities united with the copper.

Whether this explains the experimental colors or not, the idea is thought provoking.

In 1902, Weller introduced his Sicardo line — but not until 1904 was Roseville able to develop a similar line for the competitive market. John J. Herold is credited with the creation of the Rozane Mara which was regarded as a successful imitation of the jealously guarded secret formulae of Sicardo. Mara was a metallic lustre line; shapes with simple embossed designs were decorated with iridescent shades of deep magenta to rose . . . those with a smooth surface were decorated with intricate patterns of the deep magenta interwoven with pearly grey or white tones. Mara was not in production nearly as long or in such large quantities as Sicardo, and many pieces found today are unmarked.

Roseville employed Gazo Fudji (also written Foudji, Fudjiyama), a Japanese artist who had previously worked for Weller, to develop the Oriental art style of decoration that had continued to attract enthusiastic attention since being displayed in this country for the first time in 1876 at the Centennial Exposition in Philadelphia. The Company's 1905 catalogue shows the Rozane Woodland line, developed by Fudji. Woodland featured designs of naturalistic flowers and leaves, their outlines incised into the moist clay. Only the incised decorations were colored with a glossy enamel, the backgrounds left in the bisque state, and the inside glazed to hold the water. On some pieces the bisque background was further decorated with stippling, done by hand with pins used to prick the soft clay. In the 1906 catalogue, this type of decorated ware was also refered to as "Fudjiyama" and was marked with a rubber stamp in black ink with the name in print.

Rozane Fudji was a second line attributed to the artistry of Gazo Fudji. It was one of three new art lines that first appeared in the Company's 1906 catalogue. It was similar to Woodland in that the colored designs decorated a bisque background, which was usually a soft beige or a pale grey, shading to a more intense shade around the neck or at the base. Colored slip was painted on in unique, intricate patterns. Flowers were stylized; and solid lines arranged in Oriental forms were outlined with rows of dots. Beyond these were areas filled in with fields of wavy lines.

The pottery industry had always been plagued and production hampered by losses incurred in the firing process. Although usually discarded, the company attempted to market some of these pieces claiming that the unexpected action of the fire had produced results of such a beautiful and artistic nature that the value of such a piece had actually increased. Each piece was inspected after firing and priced according to its individual merit.

New techniques were developed in the laboratories that represented considerable advancement in process and control. As a result, a new line, Rozane Crystalis was developed. The crystaline glaze most often appears heavy and rough and rather sparcely studded with flat crystal flakes, although on some, smooth surfaces are covered with beautiful frost-like crystals. The heavier, rough glaze seems to have been used on the Crystalis line shapes, shown in the 1906 catalogue, the second type may have been applied to the standard Rozane shapes. Like Mongol, Rozane Crystalis met with only limited commercial success, although both represented valuable achievements to the art pottery industry. Crystalis may be marked with the Rozane Ware seal, or not at all.

Perhaps the most famous of the Roseville art lines was the Della Robbia line, introduced in 1906 by Frederick Hurten Rhead who was art director at Roseville from 1904-1908. The designs were carved into moist clay — either freehand or copied by means of a stencil. Then the background clay was cut away to reveal a second layer of color, a process called sgraffito. Other colors were added to complete the design by means of slip painting. Large pieces could require a day to complete, while smaller ones might be finished in less than two hours. A variety of motifs were shown — naturalistic as well as stylized; studies of floral and fruit arrangements; geometric patterns; pictorial scenes of Viking warriors and Roman gladiators; animals; and pieces with whimsical messages. Although seventy-five different shapes were shown in the catalogues, Della Robbia was never made in any large volume. It is marked with the Rozane Ware seal, or not at all.

Even more limited in production, the Rozane Olympic line of 1905 was strikingly reminiscent of the ancient Greek red-figure wares. Scenes from Greek mythology were copied by means of a stencil; white figures outlined in black on a red background were accented by bands of the Greek Key design. On some pieces, a caption descriptive of the scene was printed on the bottom in black ink along with the mark, ROZANE OLYMPIC POTTERY. This line is usually considered to be the rarest of the Roseville lines.

The following excerpt is from a delightfully written article by Lura Milburn Cobb (The Southwesterner's Book, Dec. 1905) in which she describes the refining of the clays and the decorating and firing processes . . . the title of the article . . . A Visit To Some Zanesville Potteries.

> We went first to the Roseville potteries, which occupy a large group of buildings, wherein is manufactured a great variety of wares, including washstand sets, jardinieres, and art ware. Over three hundred persons are employed at this plant, and about five thousand pieces of finished ware are turned out every day.
>
> As our time was limited, and we were both very fond of art pottery, my friend and I visited only the rooms in which the art ware is manufactured.
>
> Our guide led us from room to room, showing and explaining to us the various processes through which the clay passes.
>
> We learned that the Ohio clays naturally run to golden browns and yellows, that can be preserved unaltered through the intense heat of the firing to which the ware is subjected.
>
> Most of the potteries use clay from the neighboring hills, but to produce certain kinds of ware, and certain color effects, other ingredients are added; sometimes clays from other sources are used entirely or mixed with the native clays.
>
> The abundant supply of natural gas at Zanesville is a potent factor in the manufacturing of all kinds of pottery. By its use degrees of heat are attained that would be impossible by other methods of firing, and the buildings are kept clean and free from dust.
>
> Led by our guide, we viewed with interest the processes through which the clay is taken, from the time it reaches the factory, fresh from the neighboring hills, until it is transformed into a thing of beauty, fit to grace an artistic home.
>
> The clay is pulverized and thoroughly washed, filtered and mixed with water, to a certain consistency. It is then either by hand or machine, pressed into a mold made of plaster of paris. This mold absorbs the water, making a body of clay next to the mold. After three or four minutes, the liquid that remains is poured out. The shell thus left is the future vase. It goes to the finisher who sponges and smooths off all defects.
>
> The underglaze art ware is sprayed with a clay liquid in mineral colors, and the blending is done by the young girls in charge of this branch of the work. We were allowed to stand and watch the decorators at work, painting from nature or copy, in mineral colors, giving to each article with skillful fingers its own individual crown of beauty.
>
> After being decorated, the piece is taken to the dry room, where it stays until the water has all evaporated, and then is placed in the kiln.
>
> We were surprised to find how large the kilns are, some of them being twenty feet high inside. The men have to climb on ladders to put on the top of the tall columns of saggers, or boxes of clay which contain the precious ware. At the right time, after the ordeal by fire, each article is dipped in a liquid glass solution called glaze, and after this, fired for the second time, and is then a finished product.
>
> We were told that we had seen the usual process of manufacturing art ware, but variations of this and different processes are used, to produce other effects, and that the artist chemists are allowed to experiment, and often achieve wonderful results.
>
> The greatest care in every detail must be exercised in order to secure perfection.
>
> Most of the decorators were women, and I observed women and girls at work in many other rooms. Such employment must be very pleasant, congenial and suitable, bringing them into constant contact with beauty, in form and color, and it demands the care, patience and attention to detail which women are fitted by nature to give to their work.
>
> The art ware that is made at Roseville is known by the general name of Rozane ware. In the large salesrooms we saw the different kinds, each having its own peculiar charm.
>
> The first style was developed in the natural golden browns and yellows of the native clays, and is called Rozane Royal.
>
> Our attention was attracted to a collection of vases, varying in shape, in a solid color, a deep rich, beautiful red, without decorations, and we found we were viewing a unique and new variety, the Rozane Mongol, resembling the far-named Doulton ware of England.
>
> Near this stood a group of articles in soft shades of old green, reproductions in shape and decoration of antiques of Egyptian art. The attractive and restful color and the graceful modeling of decoration were harmonious and pleasing. My friend considered

this ware ideal for holding flowers, and said she could imagine how beautiful nasturtiums or carnations would look in Rozane Egypto vases.

More ornamental and striking is the Rozane Mara, whose iridescent surface seems to hold a stray rainbow imprisoned in its shining depths. The shifting opal tints, varying in tone, flushing to deepest rose, produce a beautiful play of color.

We were highly pleased with Rozane Woodland, whose exceptional beauty elicits instant praise. Gray, yellow or brown shaded backgrounds are decorated with enameled or modeled designs, usually in foliage in brown or russet autumnal hues. A Japanese artist, Gazo Foudji, formerly of Paris, does the original and exquisite work in his private studio at Roseville.

Having spent all the time at our disposal, viewing the art ware, we were obliged to hasten away from the Roseville potteries, without devoting any attention whatever to the other lines of ware manufactured there.

All of the smaller shapes and many of the larger forms were cast molded in the process described above. The very large umbrella stands and other large cylindrical pieces whose shapes lent themselves to the process, were molded by "jiggering" or "jollying." Two-part molds, strapped tightly together, were centered on the wheel and turned rapidly. The proper amount of very soft clay was thrown into the mold by the "jiggerman" and was pressed against the sides of the mold with a wooden stick or paddle until the desired thickness was obtained. The excess clay was removed and the final smoothing touches given to the interior. It was allowed to dry long enough to shrink sufficiently to be removed from the mold.

Over-molded pieces, and those not meeting Roseville's high standards of quality, were marketed as "seconds". It was standard procedure to remove or to mutilate the seal on these pieces, thereby indicating that they were second quality.

By 1905, Roseville's sales per year amounted to about $500,000. Their wares were shipped to all parts of the United States, Canada, the West Indies, and Mexico. The board of directors were: J. F. Cole of Southbend, Indiana; Samuel T. Turpin of Brooklyn, N. Y.; J. W. Baker of Frazeyburg, Ohio; and J. L. Pugh of Zanesville. George B. Emerson of Salesville, Ohio, served as President; J. F. Weaver of Roseville, as Vice President; and George F. Young continued in the capacity of Secretary, Treasurer, and General Manager.

The art lines alone, however, were by no means the basis for Roseville's success. Some lines were, at best, very limited in production; and, due to a variety of influencing economic and social changes, the market for hand decorated underglaze art pottery was on the wane early in the second decade, although it continued to be made in a very limited amount until 1919. It was their very stable commercial lines that accounted for their continuing success.

COMMERCIAL ARTWARE DEPARTMENT ESTABLISHED

In 1903, John J. Herold, superintendent of the art department, had organized an overglaze department. Several methods of decoration were used, none of which required any particular skill or talent. For instance, smoker sets, dresser sets, stein sets, and many other items were decorated with inexpensive decalcomania transfers, in such patterns as Dutch, Indian, Forget-Me-Not, and Medallion. Lines such as Tourist, Juvenile and Autumn were decorated by means of a method called "pouncing". Waxed patterns were perforated so as to allow powdered talc to sift through. Decorators simply followed the lines that adhered to the ware, adding tinted glazes as the pattern required. The third method, and the most freqently used one through the years that Roseville was in production, was first used on such lines as Chloron, Cameo, Cremo and Holland. Designs in low relief made it possible for even unskilled workers to decorate the ware by using air brushes or sponges, following the embossed lines.

We must consider that with the end of individualized hand decorating by artists left free to express their talents through their work, the era of "art" pottery, in the strictest sense, had passed. The pottery produced through the mass production methods might more correctly be referred to as "commercial art ware"; yet there is a definite creative element present — in the graceful shapes created by the modelers and in the uniquely beautiful glazes of the artisan chemists.

PAULEO FORMULAE AND COLOR COMPOSITION

When Frederick Rhead resigned his position at Roseville in 1908, his brother Harry Rhead came from England to succeed him as art director. In 1914, Rhead introduced the Pauleo line, so named for Young's daughter-in-law-Pauline and his daughter Leota. It was a prestige line, made to sell exclusively at Roseville's New York shop at Fifth Avenue and 50th Street.

It is possible to make quite a thorough study of the Pauleo line from the notebook in the Roseville files at the Historical Society in Columbus, Ohio. Written in large penciled letters on the cardboard cover are the words "PAULEO FINISHES."

The first page shows the formulae for two types of glazes. Number 1 is for a lustre finish. Number 2 is for a marbleized, or broken, cover. On a later page, we found this enlightening notation: Broken means covered with breaks and veins. With this definition in mind, the line written in at the top of the sheet is more easily understood. Plate 3 is only one of many such pages that give formulae for some 222 different color effects; some are lustre (unbroken) and some are marbleized, (broken). The L. 5 finish, mentioned twice on the first page, was written in as follows:

Plate 2

REQUISITION BLANK

MUST BE USED FOR ALL SUPPLIES WANTED

If lustre is put over a broken or cover vase do not fill in until next day.

191

The following articles are need for

Plant Dept.

Ware must be perfectly clean. Foreman

When Lustre is too thick, thin with essence.

After spraying one color, clean out airbrush thoroughly with oil of Lavender before using another color.

If finish has to be broken the Lustre can be sprayed on heavier than for a plain unbroken ground such as L.5.

No 1 cover is one teaspoonful of Epsom Salts to 1/2 pt stale beer.

No 2 cover is Hanovia's marbleizing cover.

The main finishes which are wanted in N.Y. are L.5. which is not covered and finishes covered with No.2. Cover.

Give hard fire in kiln and repeat process until color is deep and rich. After firing wash off scum with sponge and dry cloth.

Approved Gen. Mgr.

This to be charged to Account.

If color shows signs of coming off give a coat of White Lustre and fire again.

Covers should be applied about 20 minutes after Lustre.

L. 5 Brown to Orange — not broken, 2 fires or more. Note Plate 3 below, L. 64 — same as L. 5, but lighter. L. 66 gives a formula for a dark blue and brown pebble finish. Another was for a pink on pink effect, with this notation penciled in . . . "gives Carnelian glaze, undesirable." Some "freaks" were noted, evidently a combination tried only once. On a page showing several vase shapes was yet another note: Vases and finishes sent to New York — Green, Blue and Orange.

Plate 4 shows only one page of the sketches of Pauleo shapes. There were eighteen shapes in all; one was a ginger jar; one large straight-sided vase was decorated (as were several others) with dragon flys — according to the notation below. Any art work was done overglaze on the lustre cover, and the quality of the art work was not well developed.

Aztec was a slip-ware line designed by Harry Rhead about 1915. Thin threads of clay were applied to the ware much as a cake would be decorated. This squeeze bag technique had been an innovation of Frederick Hurten Rhead, and had been used earlier on some of the commerical creamware. Many pieces of Aztec are found to be artist signed.

Returning to Zanesville from a trip to his native England, Harry Rhead brought with him a jardinere that had been made in Czechoslovakia. It was decorated with cherubs in the style of the Italian sculptor,

Plate 3

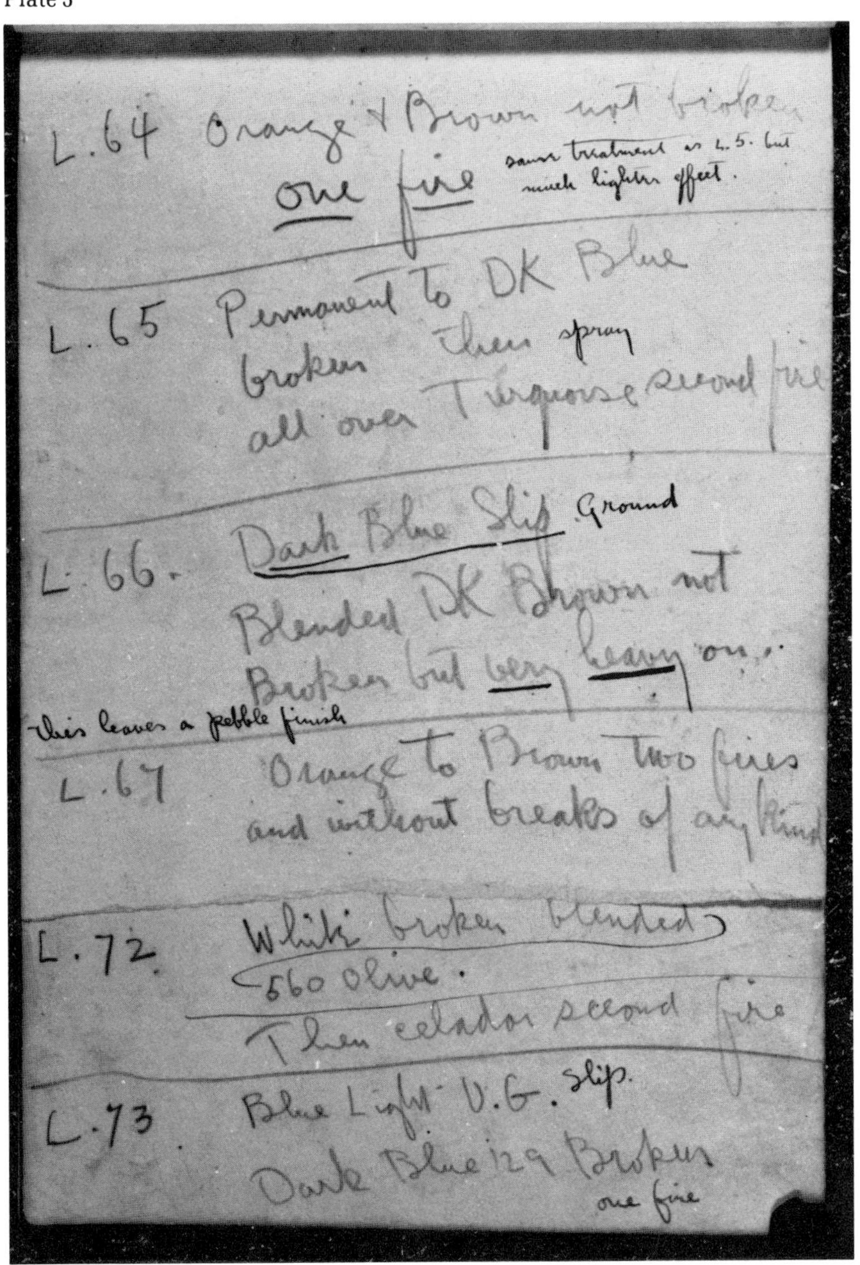
L. 64 Orange & Brown not broken
one fire same treatment as L. 5. but much lighter effect.

L. 65 Permanent to DK Blue
broken then spray
all over Turquoise second fire

L. 66. Dark Blue Slip Ground
Blended DK Brown not
Broken but very heavy on..
this leaves a pebble finish

L. 67 Orange to Brown two fires
and without breaks of any kind

L. 72 White broken blended
560 Olive.
Then celadon second fire

L. 73 Blue Light U.G. slip.
Dark Blue 129 Broken
one fire

Donatello. In 1915, Rhead introduced his Donatello line. It was an instant success and earned for both Rhead and the Roseville pottery national recognition. Plaster castings were made of Donatello figures and, by means of alternate drying and firing, were shrunken to appropriate size and used in the modeling. The Donatello line offered a hundred shapes and continued to be in popular demand for the next 10 years. Even today, it is eagerly sought by collectors.

The next years saw many changes at the pottery. In 1915, George Krause of Bunzlau, Germany, succeeded Carl E. Offinger as head of technical supervision and development. The two locations in Roseville were closed after 1910, and, in 1917, the Muskingum Avenue plant which produced the German Cookingware was destroyed by fire. The remaining location on Linden Avenue which formerly produced only art ware was enlarged, and the facilities remodeled to accommodate the increased production load. In 1918, the periodic kilns were replaced by a modern tunnel kiln, one of the first to be used in the potting industry.

The following is a portion taken from the Daily Reports of 1918 and 1919. Not every day's report is included, but the few shown here give insight to the operations at the pottery, and the problems that plagued them. Note especially the entry for February 6.

Plate 4

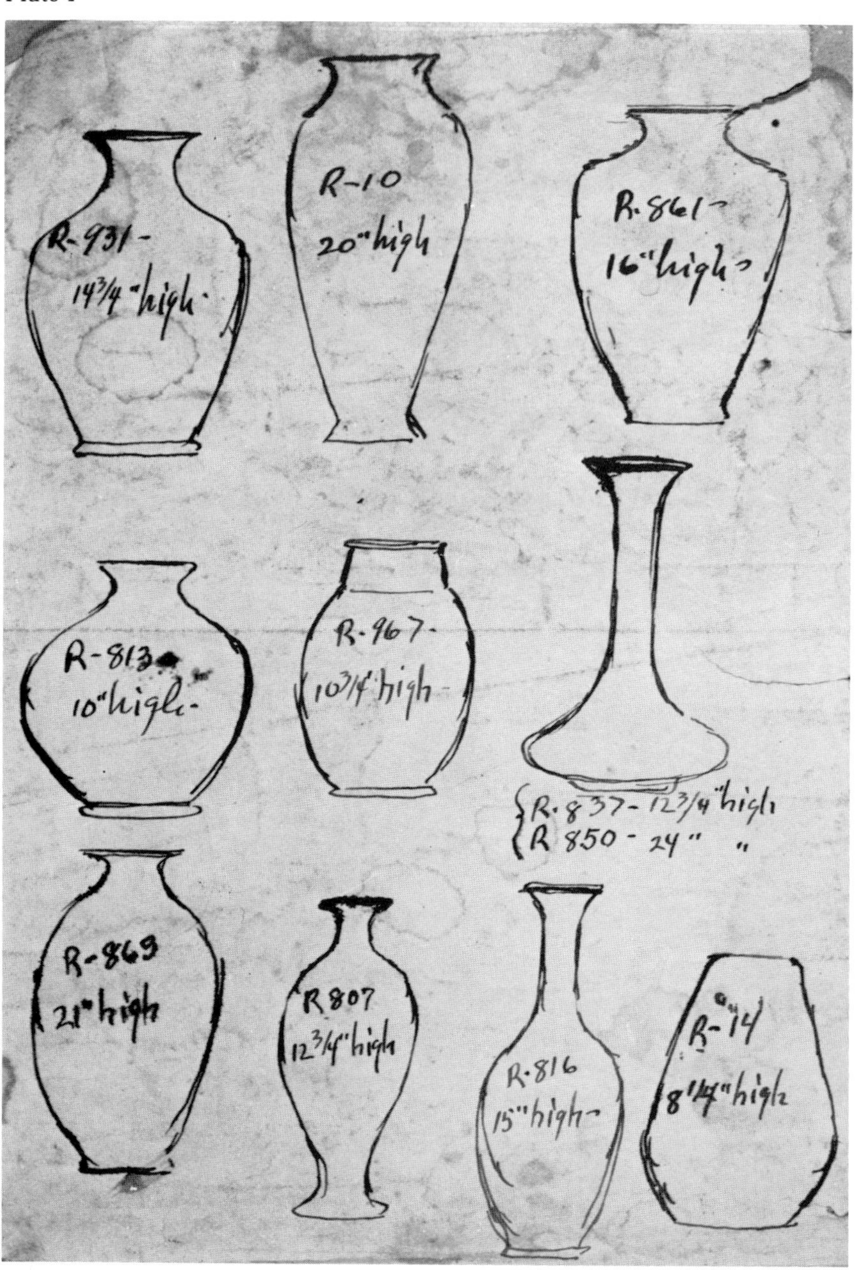

DAILY REPORTS 1918 AND 1919

At a meeting of the department heads of the company, the following duties are ascribed to these individuals: Designers, Harry H. Rhead, designing and decorating, overseeing help, supervision of decorating rooms. Wade France, responsibility and shipment of orders, ordering of molds necessary, and making and setting of ware necessary to balance orders, hiring of men, and stock of packing room. W. C. Weaver, cooking ware, making finishes and quality of same, hiring of employees in said department. Harold Johns, charge of manufacturing department, responsible for hiring employees in that department. George Krause, glazing bodies and firing; and R. T. Young, all questions of wages, employment, and general supervision.

Jan. 15, 1918: Trouble with cracking in the molds, baby plates are cracking in the bisque, tea pot lids do not fit, new molds do not fit collars, blisters in the molds, lids for pots do not fit. Wade instructed to enforce rule, not enough care in preparing clay . . . too many lumps. Caused by hot air from exhaust fan.

Jan. 19, 1918: Factory closed from war order until the 22nd. Wade . . . 934 cracked baby plates, 960 good.

Jan. 21, 1918: Cookware coming good, white bisque still cracking. George to change white body to avoid breakage in the kiln. (22nd entry shows less breakage after the change.)

Jan. 25, 1918: Cookware too hard causing dark color. Shortage of tea pots. Donatello bisque coming better. Tea pots coming better. George complains of gas pressure, must have someone responsible all time. Rhead . . . blisters from top of kiln.

Jan. 20, 1918: Streaky glazed cookware, caused by soft bisque.

Jan. 31, 1918: Two more wheelmen needed. Ware coming without cracking, try to make ware lighter. Complaints of girls going from one department to another. Rule hereafter: no one to be employed who has worked in factory to be taken on until investigated by former foreman.

Feb. 1, 1918: Baby plates bad, will try new style. Red pitchers crooked, claims due to handling green.

Feb. 4, 1918: Will have 4 wheelmen in Tuesday. No one working today, Donatello 15 good and 16 bad, 3 cracked in bottom.

Feb. 6, 1918: Started fire in tunnel kiln, no steam on the third floor. Weaver requires new wheel to make sixth wheelman.

Feb. 14, 1918: Mostique still bad outside, George is trying new glaze. 573 jars handles blew off.

Feb. 15, 1918: 1,286 baby plates bad, 535 good.

Feb. 18, 1918: Weaver in good shape, 5 wheelmen. Wade . . . cookware not hard enough, Johns needs new molds, George . . . new baby plate good.

Feb. 23, 1918: New baby plate shape ready, Weaver short girls, too soft bisque. Johns 56 body not right.

May 23, 1918: Rhead new baby plates fine, gloss very satisfactory. Weaver . . . 6 wheels making 989 teapots daily. Clay is full of dirt. Wade . . . lids not fitting.

April 19, 1918: Harold, ware coming good. Short one mold boy, sick. Will make 40% more nursery. Weaver short 4 boys, girls O.K. Unable to get men or boys. Wade . . . U S 56 body bursting, Matt white blistering. Rhead can use man in nursery and white [ware]. No. 1 mug short. No record of bad man . . . all should be reported.

April 19, 1918: Harold short 2 wheelmen and 5 girls. Wade . . . Donatello blistering and stain. Cause, not enough China clay in glaze. Weaver . . . 2 men sick, girls O.K. Rhead, Gibbs still unable to work, trying to get another man.

May 8, 1918: Weaver . . . One wheelman sick, short one mold carrier. Girls O.K. Ware fair. Harold, good shape. Wade . . . Donatello rough, everything else O.K. Redware coming slow.

June 10, 1918: Harold . . . girls can decorate 36 8″ Rozane [pattern] per day.

June 17, 1918: Harold . . . 2 wheelmen off, mold boy drafted. Weaver short 4 more boys, clay foamy. Wade, short cookware and nursery.

June 18, 1918: All in good shape. Harold . . . clay spongy. Offers to have charge of clay

of all kinds. Wade, bowls warped, 1 good out of 17 — Donatello — due to green sagers in the kiln.
June 20, 1918: Rhead working one boy and girl under age, will abide by law and dismiss all underage.
July 5, 1918: George changed glaze on Rozane. Harold . . . 2 wheelmen off; one sick, one on vacation. Offinger . . . things looking much better, 3 girls short for week.
July 8, 1918: Harold good shape, new Rozane better, bad bisque — set too green, try to avoid. Wade . . . cookware dirty, sager dirt and other things. Offinger . . . loosing cookware in kiln. Not enough room to handle line in shop.
July 9, 1918: Short girls for decorating Rozane. Short one wheelman.
July 29, 1918: Rhead, kiln man not here, short several girls, bad ware caused by lack of supervision. George thinks cooking ware not coming right. Unable to tell cause. Bad Rozane. Offinger getting along better. Still short. Wade . . . short nursery and cookware and Rozane. Short 5 girls.

The average daily wage paid to the pottery employees in 1920 was around $3.50. The nightwatchmen earned $21.00 per week and worked 12 hours per shift. The night shift tunnel kiln man earned $24.00 for the same hours.

The following procedures were posted for the workers to observe at the end of the day shift:

GIRLS: Quit working at 3:45, then clean up her place and retire to dressing room at 7 minutes til 4:00. Foremen will blow his whistle for retiring to dressing room.
MEN: Quit working at 4:30, then clean up his place and retire to top of steps at 20 minutes to 5:00. Foreman will blow his whistle for retiring to top of steps.

George Young retired in 1918, turning the position of director over to his son, Russell T. Young. Frank Ferrell replaced Harry Rhead as art director that same year and continued in that capacity until 1954. The first of over 80 lines developed by Ferrell was Sylvan. As the name implies, the mood of sylvan was characteristic of the deep woods; bisque backgrounds resembled tree bark while the enameled decorations were of leaves in a variety of species, owls, foxes, wild grapes, and many other variations. First Dogwood, Ferrell's third line, was the first of the matte glazed floral lines that was to become almost synonomous with the Roseville name.

During the years that Ferrell designed for Roseville, new floral lines were added to production at the rate of at least two a year. Ferella, introduced in 1930, was a classic line which carried Ferrell's name.

In 1932, Mrs. Anna Young, wife of George, became president of the Roseville Pottery Company, succeeding her son. The company incorporated and the firm name was changed to Roseville Pottery, Inc. The mark adopted for use during the early thirties was the name Roseville, in semi-script, cast indented into the ware. A number code added below the name indicated the shape number and the size to the nearest inch. Later, possibly as soon as 1937, the mark was changed from cast indented to cast raised, with the letters U. S. A. added.

The shaky economy of 1935 caused a drop in sales, and the Roseville company realized the need of a line they could sell in large volume. The Pine Cone samples that Ferrell had presented years before had been rejected. These discarded samples were again brought to the attention of the company, and this time were accepted. Pine Cone proved to be the most popular line ever in production. It was produced for 15 consecutive years, during which time new shapes were continuously added to the line for a total of 75 different shapes.

Following the death of Mrs. Young in 1937, her son-in-law, F. S. Clement, became president . . . a position he held until 1944. His successor was his son-in-law, Robert Windisch, who held that position until mid-year, 1953. Then, for about seven months, Frederic J. Grant, former president of the Weller Company, took office temporarily and then was again replaced by Windisch, who continued as president until the operation closed in 1954. (Donald E. Alexander, Roseville Pottery for Collectors).

From an all time high of $1,250,000 in 1945, sales began a steady decline after WW II. There were many factors that contributed to this decline . . . the market was flooded with foreign imports produced and marketed at a fraction of the cost of domestic wares and the sale of inexpensive plastic products flourished.

During the last years of production, the pottery introduced several lines with high gloss glazes attempting to revive public interest in their products. Several potteries in Ohio and West Virginia had successfully produced and marketed a type of high gloss ceramic kitchenware which proved to be very popular with the American housewives during the Forties and into the Fifties. Roseville introduced a line of this type called Mayfair. Although still retaining the artistic shapes and style for which they were famous, several pieces of the lines . . . bowls, pitchers, tea pots, etc. . . . were perhaps more utilitarian than previous lines.

In 1948, following the suggestion of the president of the firm, Robert Windisch, a high gloss line called Wincraft revived shapes from some of the old successful lines. Pine Cone, Bushberry, Cremona, Primrose, and many other lines were represented. Vases with animal motifs were shown, as were others with a contemporary flair. To the eyes of a buying public accustomed to the Roseville matte glaze, the Wincraft line with its high gloss, seemed to be only a poor imitation; and although many pieces were quite lovely and well suited to modern decor, it was never widely accepted.

In 1952, in a final attempt to re-establish a sound market, the company produced a line of oven-serve dinnerware in a modernistic design called Raymor. But a modern-day innovation of a virtually indestructable melamine plastic dinnerware had attracted the attention of American housewives. Raymor met with no success and, as a result, all operations at the Roseville pottery were discontinued. In November, 1954, the plant was sold to the Mosaic Tile Company. Today, all that remains of the fine building constructed on the Linden Avenue site is the first floor. It is now used only for storage.

The giant pottery that grew and flourished for 64 years has long since disappeared into the haze of the past, trampled under the march of progress . . . but to those who enjoy the beauty they created, the Roseville Pottery is still today unforgotten . . .

ROSEVILLE ARTISTS AND THEIR SIGNATURES

Elizabeth Ayers

Virginia Adams

M. B.

A. F. Best

Jenny Burgoon

Charles Chilcote

Anthony Dunlavy

Charles Duvall

Katie Duvall

Frank Ferrell

Gazo Fudji

M. F.

Gussie Gerwick

Goldie

John Herold

Madge Hurst

Josephine Imlay

Harry Larzelere

Claude Leffler

L. McGrath

Mignon Martineau

B. Myers

Walter Myers

W. MYERS

Lily Mitchell

LM ; Mitchell

F. M.

F. M.

Grace Neff

G. NEFF

Christian Nielson (?)

CN

Mary Pierce

M. P.

Hester Pillsbury

HP ; Pillsbury

Frederick H. Rhead

F Rhead ; F. R.

Harry Rhead

H Rhead

Lois Rhead

Helen Smith

Fred Steele

F Steele

Tot Steele

Mae Timberlake

M. T.

Sarah Timberlake

S
T

Arthur Williams

AW

ROSEVILLE'S TRADEMARKS

After 1900, when the Rozane art line was added to the commercial wares already in production, the company established a system of identification using a number code. Each series of numbers indicated the particular type of ware being produced, and each number in sequence within the series represented a shape. The numbering system was discontinued after about 1910 and not until the cast indented mark of the early thirties was it resumed. Incorporated in this and the cast raised mark that followed around 1937 was the shape number and the size to the nearest inch.

Other letters and numbers found in ink or pencil on the bottom of many pieces of the commercial art lines were used to identify specific workers doing a specialized job, such as moulding, cleaning, decorating, or inspecting. These were simply an aid to quality control.

A wide variety of marks were used during the years of production at the Roseville Pottery. Although some lines were marked in more than one manner, often the mark can be an important factor to consider, where proper identification of a line is in question . . . i.e., a novice could distinguish Florane (RV mark) from the 40's Rozane (marked Roseville, U.S.A. in relief) simply by observing the mark. As he becomes more familiar with the pottery, he would of course recognize either line simply by shape, or by the slight variation in the colors. Similarly, Panel is obviously marked RV, and Silhouette, Roseville U.S.A. in relief.

The dates given for the marks below indicate the period of greatest use; however, it is generally felt that the use of some marks extended beyond the time that a new one was developed.

Of the many unmarked pieces found today, some were never marked in any way; others originally bore a paper label.

The very early RPCo mark need not be confused with the R P C O mark used early at the Rockwood pottery, since the former was die impressed and the latter simply incised. RRPCO is not a Roseville trademark, but that of the Robinson-Ransbottom Pottery, Roseville, Ohio.

Mark 1

ROZANE
RPCo

RPCo

Die impressed mark used from 1900-1904 — (?)

Mark 2.

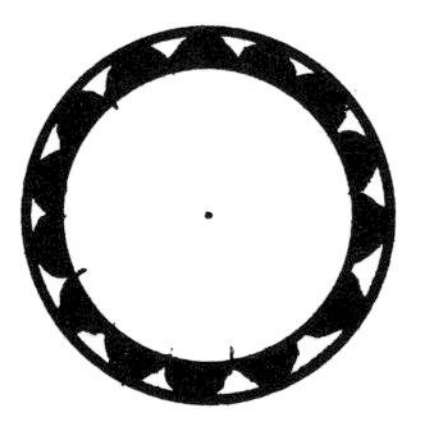

Paper sticker, printed in red ink; applied at the pottery; indicated stock number and retail price.

Mark 3.

AZUREAN

AZUREAN
RPCo

Die impressed, 1902 — (?)

Mark 4.

Applied ceramic disk, 1904 — (?)

Mark 5.

Applied ceramic seal, 1904, 05 —

Mark 6.

Fujiyama Fujiyama

Black ink stamp, 1906

Mark 7.

ROZANE
"OLYMPIC"
POTTERY

Black ink stamp or printed, often includes description of mythological scene. 1905

Mark 8.

Chloron

Ink Stamp, 1907

Mark 9.

Usually ink stamped, occasionally impressed. 1910-28

Mark 10.

ROSEVILLE
POTTERY CO.
ZANESVILLE, O.

Red ink stamp, 1910 — (?)

Mark 11.

Applied ceramic seal, 1914 —

Mark 12.

Impressed, 1915 —

Mark 13.

Ink stamp, 1917

Mark 14.

Black paper sticker, 1914-33

Mark 15.

Silver or gold paper sticker, 1930-37

Mark 16.

Roseville
915-5"

Roseville
U.S.A.

Impressed mark, 1932-37

Mark 17.

Roseville
U.S.A.

R U.S.A.

R
U.S.A.

In relief, 1937-53

Mark 18.

Lotus

In relief, 1951

Mark 19.

ROSEVILLE
L-23
PASADENA PLANTER
U.S.A.

In relief, 1952

Mark 20.

152 L
raymor
by Roseville
U.S.A.
OVENPROOF
PAT. PENd.

In relief, 1952

LINE DESCRIPTIONS AND APPROXIMATE DATES OF PRODUCTION

** indicates catalogue reprint*

Antique Matt Green, before 1916. Simple shades in matte green glaze with areas that have a burnished or rusty appearance.

Apple Blossom, 1948. Spray of white blossoms on backgrounds of pink, blue, green . . . brown tree branches form graceful handles.

Autumn, before 1916. Creamware decorated by means of pouncing. Shades of rose to green depicting trees and country side. *

Aztec, 1916. Simple decorations formed with thin threads of clay using a squeeze-bag technique.

Azurean, 1902. Blue and white underglaze art ware on a blue blended background.

Azurine, Orchid, and Turquoise, 1920. Simple shapes, very similar to Lustre line, high gloss, lustrous glaze.*

Baneda, 1933. Decorative band of leaves, pods, and blossoms on backgrounds of red, green, and more rarely, blue.

Banks, early 1900's. Novelties and banks in the forms of a cat, Uncle Sam, pigs, dog, buffalo, and eagle . . . poorly hand decorated under glaze.*

Bittersweet, 1940. Orange pods and green leaves, with twig handles on backgrounds of mint green, grey, or yellow.

Blackberry, 1933. Band of berries, vines and leaves in natural colors, on green rough-textured background.

Bleeding Heart, 1938. Pink blossoms and green foliage on backgrounds of shaded pink or blue.

Blue Ware, 1910. Underglaze artist decorated, in shades of medium to dark blue. (School of thought is divided on this line . . . some consider it a bona fide Roseville production; others do not. We can find no reference to it in the Roseville files. The only marked piece we are aware of is pictured in the following color plates; however, it is marked with a paper label.)

Burmese, 1950's. Oriental faces decorate such items as wall plaques, book-ends, candleholders, console bowls, etc. Colors are green, black and white.

Bushberry, 1948. Leaves and berries on bark-like backgrounds of green, blue, or russet.

Cameo, 1920. Antique ivory bands with embossed figures and trees, or vertical panel with peacock, on dark green or ivory backgrounds.*

Carnelian I, 1910-15. The ornate handles are characteristic of the line, and should be considered as a point of identification. There are two distinct types of glaze on these shapes . . . (A) is a smooth matte glaze, with a drip glaze in a darker shade; colors are light with medium blue; aqua blue with turquoise; pink with blue; green with antique gold. (B) is heavy and textured, rose, black, purple and yellow glazes are intermingled and show some running; found occasionally in shades of turquoise.

Carnelian II, 1915. Intermingled color effect; drip glaze on some shapes, no common characteristic.* Note: Although it is generally accepted that there were indeed two Carnelian lines . . . in our observations and studying we found we had three! In addition to the two types described above in the Carnelian I lines, we found in the catalogue another line listed as Carnelian, but whose shapes were in no way similar to the others. Since we occasionally found different glaze treatments within the same line . . . i.e. Topeo, Tourmaline, Crystallis . . . we classed the first two types as Carnelian I, since they were identically modeled, and the third as Carnelian II. This catalogue reprint is on page 151.

Ceramic Design, before 1916. Creamware, usually embossed designs in colors of yellow, green, and black. However, catalogues show a repetitive border type pattern, applied by the pouncing technique in bright colors, which is referred to as Persian type Ceramic Design.

Cherry Blossom, 1933. Blue with pink lattice, yellow with brown lattice, sprigs of cherry blossoms, and twigs.

Crystal Green, 1930's. See page 147 for possible identification.

Chloron, 1907. Solid matte green glaze, sometimes with sections in ivory, modeled in high relief after early Roman and Greek pottery artifacts.*

Clemana, 1934. Basketweave backgrounds of green, blue, or tan, with stylized blossoms and leaves.

Clematis, 1944. Clematis blooms on backgrounds of Autumn Brown, Ciel blue, or Forest Green.

Colonial, 1900's. Glossy spongeware in shades of blue, with gold highlights on embossed detail at base of handles.*

Columbine, 1940. Floral and leaf arrangement on shaded backgrounds of tan, blue, or pink.

Commercial line, 1940's. Line of planters, in a variety of shapes and color combinations. Some are square or rectangular, embossed with swirls, others are twisted. Colors are lime green with tan; turquoise with tan; and solid tan.

Corinthian, 1923. Deep vertical ivory fluting with green in recessed areas; green band decorated with twisted grape vines, leaves and fruit in natural colors; further embellished by a finely modeled narrow band in ivory and green.

Cornelian, early 1900's. Glossy spongeware in shades of yellow and brown, accented with random areas of gold spray. *

Cosmos, 1940. Delicate flowers and greenery on suggestion of a band, textured background colors are blue, green, or tan.

Cremo, 1916. Shades from rose at the top, through yellow to dark green at the bottom. Characterized by vertical, evenly spaced, swirling stems with single blossom in blue. *

Cremona, 1927. Floral motif varies . . . some pieces have single tall stem with small blossoms and several arrowhead leaves; others are wreathed with leaves similar to Velmoss; a third variety is a web of delicate vines; characteristic glaze has a buttermilk, or curdled effect; backgrounds are light green mottled with pale blue, or pink with creamy ivory. There is also a medium green, with less texture than the other colors, and you may find still other shades.

Crystalis, Rozane, 1906. Unique shapes, some with extreme handles; many are three-footed; textured glaze with scattered crystal flakes, or standard Rozane shapes with smooth surface and grown crystals, rare. Also see text. *

Dahlrose, 1924-28. Mottled tan background with band formed by ivory flowers and green leaves.

Dawn, 1937. Simple incised floral decoration; long slender petals, no leaves; backgrounds are pink, yellow, or blue.

Decorated Utility Ware, 1920. Creamware with high gloss, some decorated with wide bands of green or orange, narrowly piped in black; another type is decorated with slender blue leaves and orange berries.

Della Robbia, Rozane, 1906. Naturalistic or stylized designs executed by hand using the sgraffito method. Also see text. *

Dogwood I, 1918. Textured green background with white dogwood blossoms on brown branches.

Dogwood II, 1928. Smooth green background with white dogwood blossoms on black branches.

Donatella Tea Sets, before 1916. This term referred to tea sets, consisting of tea pot, sugar and creamer, in a variety of patterns, such as Landscape, Ceramic, Forget-Me-Not, Medallion, and others.*

Donatello, 1915. Deep vertical fluting in ivory and green, on either side of a brown band with embossed ivory cherubs and trees. Catalogue also shows grey and ivory combination. Also see text.

Dutch, before 1916. Creamware with decals of varied scenes with Dutch children; trimmed with narrow blue piping at the rim.

Earlam, 1930. Turquoise matte, with glossy mottled effect, lined in tan. Included in this line were many crocus pots, in tan and green matte glaze. *

Early Pitchers, before 1916. High gloss, utility line of pitchers with various embossed scenes. Shown are The Bridge; The Cow; The Boy; The Golden Rod; The Wild Rose; The Mill; The Grape; No. I Holland; No. II Holland; Teddy Bear; Iris; Tulip; Landscape; and Owl. *

Egypto, Rozane, 1905. Matte glaze in soft shade of old green, modeled from examples of ancient Egyptian pottery.

Elsie, the Cow. Advertising line made for Borden's; consists of mug, cereal bowl and plate with embossed decorations of Elsie, the Cow; in high gloss tan glaze.

Falline, 1933. Blended backgrounds of tan shading to green and blue, or tan to darker brown; evenly curving panels are separated by vertical "pea-pod" decorations.

Ferella, 1931. Brown or rose curdled glaze effect; decorated with bands of stylized shells and cut-outs around the rim and base.

Florane, 1920's. Shaded matte glaze of carmel tan to very dark brown on simple shapes, often from the Rosecraft line.

Florentine, 1924-28. Brown bark textured panels alternating with perpendicular stripes embossed with cascades of leaves and berries, also brown. Found occasionally in ivory with green cascades and brown textured panels.

Florentine II, after 1937. Similar to the ivory Florentine, but without cascades on the dividing panels, marked Roseville, U.S.A. in relief.

Forget-Me-Not, before 1916. Creamware decorated with decals of small blue or lavender flowers, with gold piping.

Forest, 1920's (?) Unidentified line, see page 147.

Foxglove, 1940's. Tall spires of flowers in delicate colors, on backgrounds of shaded pink, blue, and green.

Freesia, 1945. Floral clusters, blade-like leaves on shaded backgrounds of Tropical Green, Delft Blue, and Tangerine.

Fudji, Rozane, 1906. Bisque backgrounds in tones of grey or beige, decorated with colored slip in unique, intricate patterns. Also see text.

Fuschia, 1939. Vine with serrated leaves and delicate blooms on highlighted backgrounds of blue, tan, or Forest green.

Futura, 1928. Very diversified line; some forms are angular, suggesting a geometric or Art Deco feeling; some suggest lines of the future . . . Pine Cone, Teasel, and others; some are decorated with leaves in various colors. Typical glaze is matte, although an occasional piece may be high-gloss.*

Garden Pottery, 1931. Stoneware, pots, jardinieres, and bird baths, with a variety of embossed decorations. *

Gardenia, 1940's. White gardenia, green leaves, on slightly textured, shaded backgrounds of Seafoam, Golden tan, and Silver Haze grey.

German Cooking Ware, 1912. Utilitarian line; brown lined in white, decorated with a border of scallops at the top. This line contained such items as coffee pots, tea pots, pitchers, custard or bean pots, casseroles, shirred egg cups, pudding dishes, mixing bowls, etc.

Gold Traced, before 1916. Candleholders, candlelabra, etc., in white with delicate gold patterns. *

Decorated and Gold Traced, before 1916. Same as Gold Traced, but with added floral motif, similar to Persian. Listed in this manner in old price list. *

Holland, before 1916. Dutch figures are embossed on an ivory background, shaded green around the rim and base. *

Holly, before 1916. Creamware with decal of holly leaves and red berries with narrow piping at the rim.

Imperial I, 1916. Pretzel-twisted vine and stylized grape leaves decorate rough textured background in green and brown. Style of modeling is rather crude.

Imperial II, 1924. Much variation within the line. There is no common characteristic, although many pieces are heavily glazed, and colors tend to run and blend.*

Individual tea sets, before 1916. Decorated creamware in such various patterns as Ceramic Design, Medallion, Dutch, Forget-Me-Not, Landscape, in sets containing the tea pot, sugar and creamer.

Iris, 1938. White Iris, green blades on blended backgrounds of blue, pink or carmel tan.

Ivory II, 1937. White matte glazed shapes from earlier lines such as Orian, Velmoss, Russco, Donatello, Tourmaline and others. Also included in the line is a figurine of a nude with flowing drapery, and another of a sleeping dog, also in white. *

Old Ivory, before 1916. (Also called Ivory Frieze) Intricate patterns in high relief of stylized grape vines, or flowers; also was made in delicate colors of pink, blue, and green. When these tints were used, the color was wiped from the areas in highest relief, and was usually referred to as green tint, blue tint, etc.*

Ixia, 1930's. Delicate floral cluster on stem; shaded background colors are yellow, pink and green. Closed, pointed handles were characteristic.

Jeanette, before 1916. Creamware decorated with decal of standing girl in period costume.

Jonquil, 1931. White jonquil clusters and green leaves on textured brown background, lined in green.

Juvenile, before 1916- (?) Creamware, decorated by means of pouncing (perforated waxed pattern) in various motifs — chicks, bunnies, on matt glaze; duck with hat, sunbonnet girl, rabbit with jacket, pig with hat, dancing cat with parasol, etc., on high gloss. (1918 issue.)*

Landscape, 1910. Creamware decorated with decals of windmills and sailing boats, in blue and brown.

La Rose, 1924. Ivory background wreathed with swags of green vines caught up with small red roses. Beaded border at rim.

Laurel, 1934. Background colors are persimmon or old gold both accented with black; or in shades of turquoise. Wide panels symetrically divided by three impressed vertical ribs are wreathed with laurel branches.

Lombardy, 1924. Solid colors of green or blue are characterized by narrow, perpendicular panels tapering to a common point at center bottom. *

Lotus, 1952. Pointed spires of stylized leaves surround each piece. High gloss glaze in combinations of maroon with beige; brown with beige; and turquoise with beige.

Luffa, 1934. Backgrounds are green or brown, with horizontal wavy lines, decorated by a border of several small flowers and two large leaves with long points extending downward.

Lustre, 1921. Simple shapes with lustrous glaze in pink, orange, and blue. *

Magnolia, 1940. Magnolia blossoms on black stem, textured backgrounds are green, blue and tan.

Mara, Rozane, 1904. Metallic lustre line, similar to Sicardo. Intricate patterns on smooth surface in magenta and silver grey; simple embossed designs in iridescent shades of rose to magenta. Also see text.

Matt Color, 1920's (?) Simple paneled designs of various types, in colors of light blue, turquoise, yellow and pink. Later issued in high gloss in a variety of colors. *

Matt Green, before 1916. Matte green glaze on smoking set, jardinieres, fern dishes, hanging baskets, planters . . . some smooth with no pattern; some embossed with leaves, children's faces, spaced evenly around the top.

Mayfair, late 40's. Hi gloss glaze, utilitarian line, in beige, brown with tan, dark green with tan, and lime.

Medallion, before 1916. Creamware decorated with delicate gold decals around rims, and evenly spaced rose or green mercury head medallions.

Ming Tree, 1947. High gloss glaze in mint green, turquoise, or white is decorated with ming branch; handles are formed from gnarled branches.

Mock Orange, 1950. Small cluster of white blossoms and green leaves on backgrounds of pink, yellow, or mint green.

Moderne, 1930's. Blue; turquoise highlighted with gold, ivory with pink, or brown with green; unique modeling, simple decorations. *

Mongol, Rozane, 1904. High gloss blood red line on typical Chinese vase forms. Also see text.

Monticello, 1931. Black and white stylized trumpet flower evenly spaced, extending from brown ribbon-like band, Turquoise background with tan blush, brown with tan.

Morning Glory, 1935. Delicately colored blossoms and twining vines in white or green with blue.

Moss, 1930's. Green moss hanging over brown branch with green leaves, backgrounds are pink, ivory or tan, shading to blue.

Mostique, 1915. Indian designs of stylized flowers and arrowhead leaves, slip decorated on bisque, glazed interiors. Occasional bowl glazed on outside as well.

Normandy, 1924. Green and white vertical fluting over bottom portion, wide brown band, decorated with ivory looped vines, pink grapes and green leaves around rim.

Novelty Steins, before 1916. Line of creamware mugs, decorated with decals with whimsical scenes and messages. *

Olympic, Rozane, 1905. White figures outlined in black on a red background accented by bands of the Greek Key design, depicting scenes from Greek mythology. Also see text.

Opaque enamels, 1900. Simple jardinieres in plain colors of yellow, rose, and green.

Orian, 1935. Characterized by handles formed on bladelike leaves with suggestion of berries at base of handle . . . high gloss glaze; blue or tan with darker drip glaze forming delicate band around rim, or in plain yellow with no over drip.

Panel 1920. Background colors are dark green or dark brown, decorations embossed within the recessed panels are of natural or stylized floral arrangements, or female nudes.

Pasadena Planter, 1952. High gloss pink or black, with border at rim formed by white drip glaze; line consists of a variety of shapes of flower containers or planters in modern shapes.

Pauleo, 1914. Prestige line of 222 color combinations and two glaze types . . . lustre or marbleized. See text.

Peony, 1930. Floral arrangement with green leaves on textured, shaded backgrounds in yellow with brown; pink with blue; and green.

Persian, 1916. Creamware decorated by means of pouncing technique, in bright colors, Water lily and pad most common motif, although a variety of others were also used.

Pine Cone, 1931. Graceful needles and pine cones decorate backgrounds of brown, green, or blue. Handles are formed from branches. Pink background extremely rare.

Poppy, 1930. Shaded backgrounds of blue or pink with decoration of poppy flower and green leaves.

Primrose, 1932. Cluster of single blossoms on tall stems, low pad-like leaves, backgrounds are blue, tan, or pink.

Raymor, 1952. Modernistic design, oven serve dinnerware made in colors of tan, ivory, grey, dark green, black and medium green.

Rosecraft Black, 1916. Simple shapes, high gloss black glaze. *

Rosecraft, 1916-19. Simple shapes in glossy glazes, colors are yellow, dark blue, light blue, and rose. *

Rosecraft Hexagon, 1924. Shapes are six-sided, simple medallion design with long slender stylized leaf extending downward. Colors are dark green; brown with orange; catalogue also shows blue.

Rosecraft Vintage, 1924. Dark brown backgrounds with band at shoulder formed by repetitive arrangement of leaves, vines, and berries, in colors of beige to orange.

Rozane, 1900. Dark blended backgrounds; slip decorated underglaze art ware. Also see text.

Rozane, 1917's. Honeycomb backgrounds in ivory, light green, pink, yellow, blue; decorated with green leaves and clusters of roses in delicate tints.

Rozane pattern, 1940's Solid or blended matte glazes on simple shapes. Shaded browns or blues; ivory; turquoise. *

Rozane Royal, Royal Lights, 1904. With the addition of the new art lines, in 1904, the name Rozane was changed to Rozane Royal, to distinguish the underglaze artist decorated line from the other lines. Also at this time, the Royal Lights were added; slip decorated underglaze in lighter shades of grey, blue, green, ivory, pink, etc. See text.

Royal Capri, late line. Occasional pieces with modern forms, having a textured gold surface.

Russco, 1930's. Octagonal rim openings, stacked handles, narrow perpendicular panel front and back. One type glaze is solid matte color; another is matte color with lustrous crystalline over glaze, some of which show actual grown crystals.

Savona, 1924-28. High gloss glaze of salmon pink, light blue, or lime green on finely modeled classic shapes, some with deeply fluted areas around the base or near the top, with the remaining smooth areas decorated with cascading grape vines in high relief. *

Silhouette, 1952. Recessed area silhouettes nature study, or female nudes. Colors are rose, turquoise, tan and white with turquoise.

Smoker sets, before 1916. Tobacco jars, ashtrays, etc., on a tray in a variety of patterns, such as Dutch, Holland, Matte Green, Ivory Frieze, and the Tints, and Indian.

Snowberry, 1946. Brown branch with small white berries and green leaves embossed over spider-web design in various background colors . . . blue, green, and rose.

Stein Sets, before 1916. Creamware tankards and steins decorated with various decals of Dutch, Eagle, Elk, Moose, Indian, Monk, and K of P. Also included were Holland, and Ivory Frieze, and the Tint colors, green, pink, yellow, and blue. Others were hand painted.

Sunflower, 1930. Tall stems support yellow sunflowers whose blooms form a repetitive band. Textured background shades from tan to dark green at base.

Sylvan, 1918. Tree bark textured background, incised with decorations of maple leaves, dogs, chickens, foxes, owls, ivy and acorns. Interiors are glazed. *

Teasel, 1936. Emobssed decorations of long-stems, gracefully curving, with delicate spider-like pods. Colors and glaze treatments vary from monochrome matte, to crystalline. Colors are beige to tan; medium blue highlighted with gold; pale blue; and deep rose . . . possibly others.

Thorn Apple, 1930. White trumpet flower with leaves reverses to thorny pod with leaves. Colors are shaded blue, brown, and pink.

Topeo, 1934. Simple forms decorated with four vertical evenly spaced cascades of leaves in high relief at their origin, tapering downward to a point. A light green crystalline glaze shades to a mottled medium blue, with cascades in alternating green and pink. A second type is done completely in a high gloss dark red.

Tourist, before 1916. Glossy creamware decorated by means of a perforated wax stencil (pouncing) depicting a touring car on the way to an inn. Vases in three sizes, 8", 9", and 12" and a spittoon are shown in the catalogues.

Tourmaline, 1933. Although the semi-gloss medium blue, highlighted around the rim with lighter high gloss and gold effect, seems to be accepted as the standard Tourmaline glaze, the catalogue definitely shows this and two other types as well. One is a mottled overall turquoise, the other a mottled salmon which appears to be lined in the high gloss, but with no over run to the outside. *

Tuscany, 1927. Marble-like finish most often found in a shiny pink, sometimes in matte grey, more rarely in a dull turquoise. Suggestion of leaves and berries, usually at the base of handles are the only decorations.

Velmoss, 1935. Characterized by three horizontal wavy lines around the top from which long, blade-like leaves extend downward. Colors are green, blue, tan and pink.

Velmoss Schroll, 1916. Incised pattern is cut into ivory background; added colors are in the incised lines only, red roses, green leaves, and brown branches.

Victorian Art Pottery, 1924-28. Simple shapes, lightly embossed, slip decorated designs, probably meant to emulate Della Robbia. *

Venetian, early 1900's. Utilitarian ware; crockery type; in blue or yellow outside, lined with white. *

Volpato, 1918. Finely modeled, classic forms, fluted either at the top or the base, or not at all. Much variation in the line; some pieces show garlands of vines and small roses, sometimes caught up by a grape leaf. Tall pieces have cascades of flowers.

Water Lily, 1940's. Water lily and pad in various color combinations . . . tan to brown with yellow lily; blue with white lily; pink to green with pink lily.

White Rose, 1940's. Spray of white roses and green leaves on shaded backgrounds of blue; brown to green; and pink to green.

Wincraft, 1948. Revived shapes from older lines such as Pine Cone, Bushberry, Cremona, Primrose, and others. Vases with animal motif, contemporary shapes in high gloss of blue, tan, lime, and green.

Windsor, 1931. Brown or blue mottled glaze, some with leaves, vines, and ferns; some with a repetitive band arrangement of small squares and rectangles in yellow and green.

Wisteria, 1933. Roughly textured backgrounds shading from brown to deep blue, more rarely in only brown, decorated with green vine and lavender wisteria.

Woodland, Rozane, 1905. Stippled bisque backgrounds with incised decorations of naturalistic flowers and leaves colored with glossy enamel. Also see text.

Zephyr Lily, 1940's. Tall lilies and slender leaves adorn swirl-textured backgrounds of Bermuda blue, Evergreen, and Sienna Tan.

ROZANE, 1900's

Row 1:

Bowl, 2½″, Shape No. 927, marked ROZANE, RPCo.
Bud vase, w/h, 4″, Shape No. 862, marked ROZANE, RPCo.
Vase w/h, 4″, marked with the Rozane Ware Seal.
Bowl, 2½″, Shape No. 927, marked ROZANE, RPCo.

Row 2:

Ewer, 11″, Shape No. 870-4, marked ROZANE, RPCo.
Commemorative vase, 5″, Shape No. 923, marked ROZANE, RPCo.
Ewer, 7″, Shape No. 828, marked ROZANE, RPCo.
Same as above.

Row 3:

Jug, 4½″, Shape No. 888, marked ROZANE, RPCo.
Pillow vase, 9″, Shape No. 882, marked ROZANE, RPCo., Artist signed: F. Steele
Vase, 4″, Shape No. 844, marked ROZANE, RPCo., artist signed: F.R.

Row 4:

Vase, 9½″, Shape No. 821, marked ROZANE, RPCo.
Vase, 14″, marked with the Rozane Ware Seal, artist signed: Mitchell
Vase, 9½″, Shape No. 821, marked ROZANE, RPCo.

Note: Sizes are to the nearest half inch, w/h indicates "with handles."

Plate 5

ROZANE, ROZANE ROYAL

Row 1:

Vase w/h, 4″, marked with the Rozane Royal Seal
Jug, 7″, marked with the Rozane Royal Seal
Artist Signed: J. Imlay
Pitcher, 5″, Rozane Ware Seal,
Artist Signed: Mae Timberlake
Paper Weight, Rozane Ware Seal,
Artist Signed: Grace Neff
Ewer, 8″, marked ROZANE, RPCo., no art work.
Tobacco jar, 6″, Rozane Royal Seal,
Artist Signed: Walter Myers
Pitcher, 4″, ROZANE, RPCo.

Row 2:

Vase, 6½″, Rozane Royal Seal
Artist Signed: Virginia Adams
Vase, 6″, Rozane Royal
Artist Signed: J. Imlay
Vase, 10″, Rozane Royal Seal
Artist Signed: Walter Myers
Pitcher, 7″, Rozane Ware Seal
Artist Signed: Mary Pierce
Vase, 9″, marked with the Rozane Ware Seal
Vase, 8″, Rozane Royal Seal, Artist Signed: Mae Timberlake

Row 3:

Tankard, 11½″, Rozane Royal Seal, Artist Signed: J. Imlay
Vase, 14″, Rozane Royal Seal, Artist Signed: J. Imlay
Vase, 5″, Rozane Ware Seal, Artist Signed: Grace Neff
Vase, 16″, Rozane Royal Seal, Artist Signed: J. Imlay
Pillow Vase, 10 × 10″, Rozane Royal Seal
Artist Signed: Walter Myers

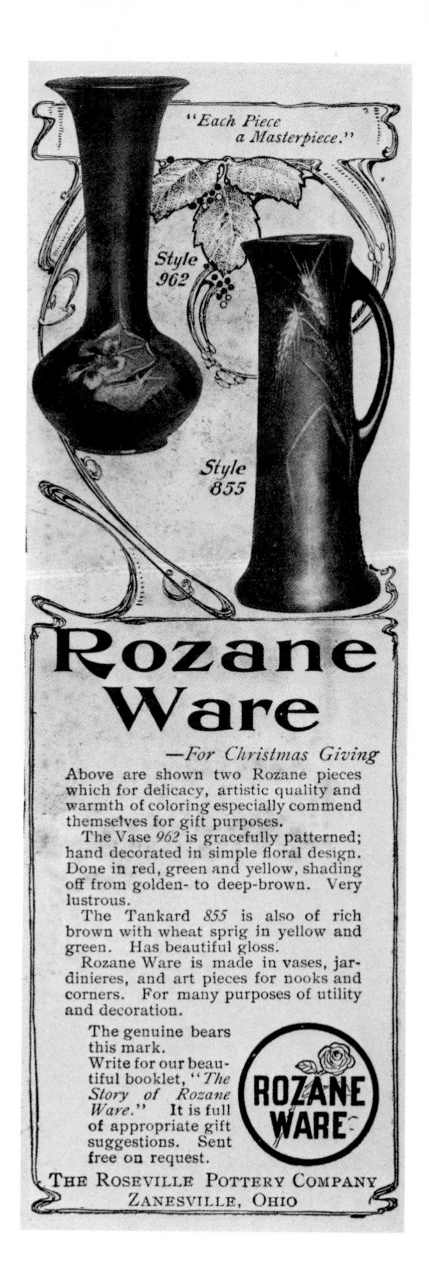

Plate 6

ROZANE, ROZANE ROYAL

Row 1:

Bud Vase, 8″, Shape No. 842, marked ROZANE, RPCo.
Vase, w/h, 6″, Shape No. 883, ROZANE, RPCo., artist signed
Vase, 9″, marked with the Rozane Royal Seal
Artist Signed: Pillsbury
Bud Vase, 6″, Shape No. 831, marked ROZANE, RPCo.
Urn, with lid, 7½″, Shape No. 901, ROZANE, RPCo.

Row 2:

Mug, 4½″, Shape No. 886, marked ROZANE, RPCo.
Artist Signed: Harry Rhead
Vase, 7″, marked with the Rozane Ware Seal
Bowl, w/h, marked with the Rozane Royal Seal
Vase, 5½″, Shape No. 853, ROZANE, RPCo., artist signed

BLUE WARE, 1910 (?)

Bottom,
Left:

Vase, 5½″, marked with Black paper label

AZUREAN, 1902

Bottom,
Center:

Vase, w/h, 4½″, marked RPCO, Artist Signed: Virginia Adams

CORNELIAN, EARLY 1900's

Bottom,
Right:

Cracker jar and lid, no mark

Plate 7

Plate 8

Plate 9

ROZANE

Jardiniere and Pedestal, 31″ overall
Shape No. 524, marked ROZANE, RPCo.

EGYPTO, 1905

Left to Right:

Oil Lamp, 5″, marked with Egypto seal
Vase, 11″, same mark
Compote, 9″, same mark
Pitcher, 5″, same mark

Plate 10

Plate 11

MARA, 1904

Top,
Left:

Vase, 13½", no mark

MONGOL, 1904

Top,
Right:

Vase, 15", marked with the Mongol Seal

Bottom,
Left:

Bowl vase, 3", marked with the Mongol Seal
Vase, 10", marked with the Rozane Ware Seal
Pitcher, 6½", marked with the Mongol Seal

CRYSTALIS, 1906

Bottom,
Right:

Ewer, 7½", marked with the Rozane Ware seal

Plate 12

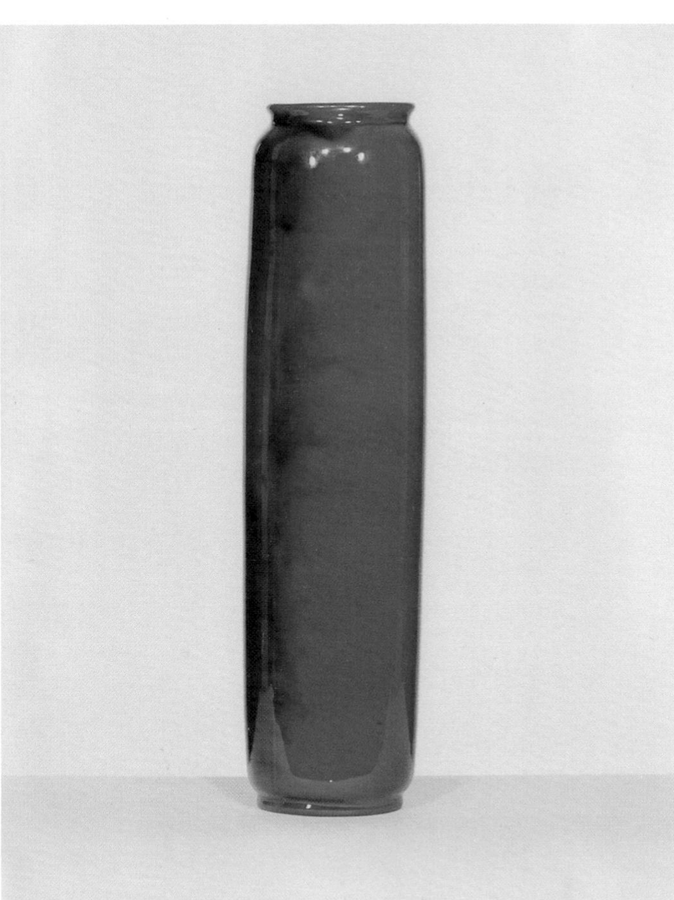

Plate 13

Plate 14

Plate 15

WOODLAND, 1905

Top,
Left to Right:

Vase, 8″, no mark
Vase, 10″, marked with the Rozane Ware Seal
Vase, 9″, marked with the Rozane Ware Seal

On Front
Cover:

Vase, 17″, marked with the Rozane Ware, Woodland Seal
Artist Signed: E. D.

FUDJI, 1906

Bottom,
Left to Right:

Vase, 9″, no mark
Vase, 10″, no mark

On Front
Cover:

Vase, 9″, marked with the Rozane Ware Seal

Plate 16

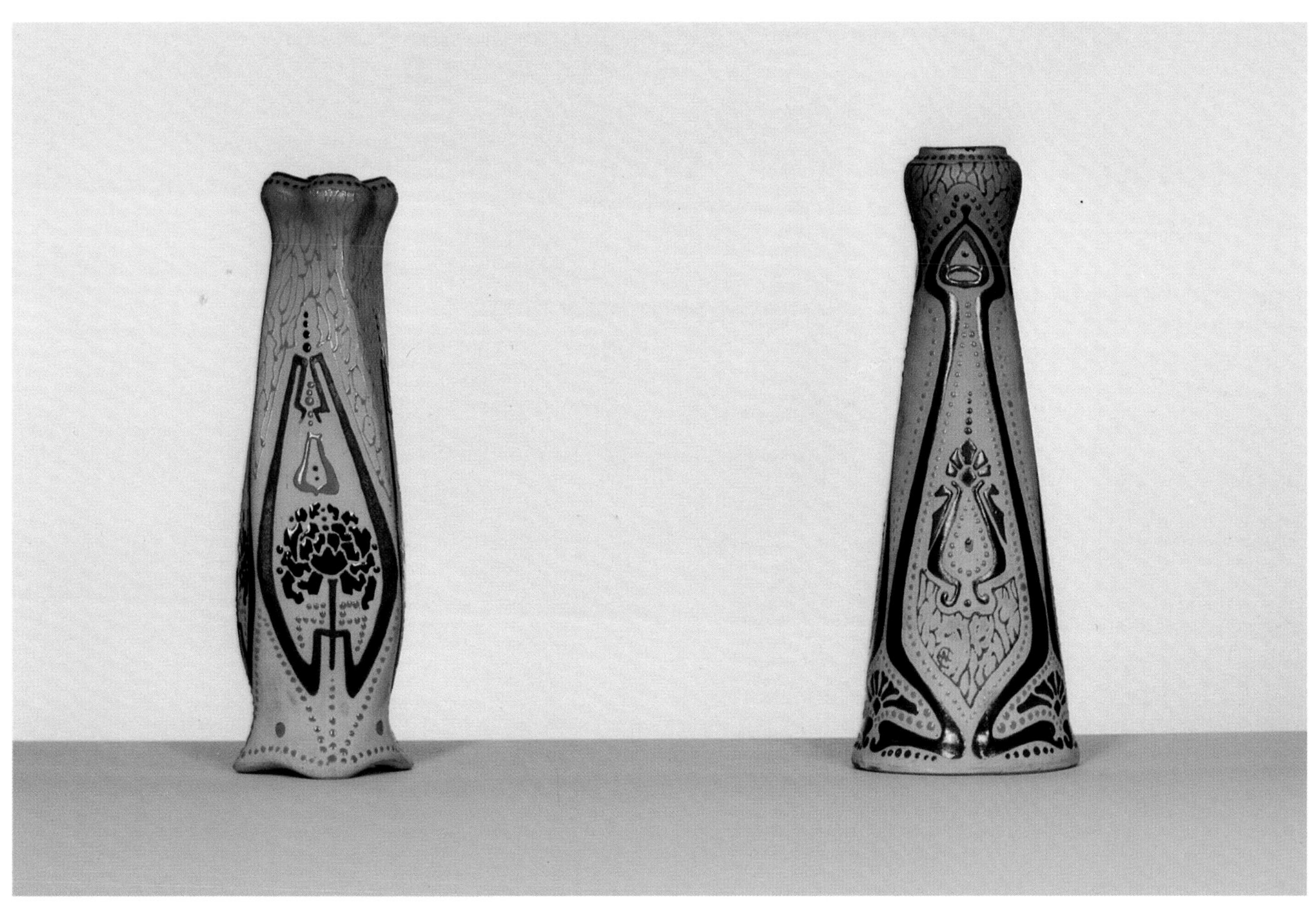
Plate 17

OLYMPIC, 1905

Top,
Left:

Vase, 13″, stamped ROZANE POTTERY, in black ink

Top,
Right:

Tankard, 11″, in black ink, Triptalemos and a Grain of Wheat.
Also, ROZANE POTTERY stamped in black

PAULEO, 1914

Vase, 20″, no mark.

When we purchased this vase, with it came this interesting and enlightening letter, signed by a former employee of the Roseville Company. The girls who were working on the line at the time these vases were made each had the opportunity to buy one, and this vase had been in this lady's home since that time.

> "This unusual piece of decorated Pauleo was manufactured by the Roseville Pottery Company of Zanesville, Ohio, in 1918 or 1919. Total production of these vases did not exceed over seventy-five or eighty. They were distributed by a firm in New York City and sold for $75.00 when originally manufactured. Miss Gray was the decorator of this piece."

DELLA ROBBIA, 1906.

Bottom,
Right:

Vase, 13″, marked with the Rozane Ware Seal

Plate 18

Plate 19

Plate 20

Plate 21

TOURIST, before 1916

Top,
Left:

Vase, 12″, no mark

MATT COLOR, 1916

Top,
Right:

Bowl, w/h, 4″, no mark
Hanging basket, 4½″, no mark
Bowl, 3″, no mark

AZTEC, 1916

Center,
Row 1:

Pitcher, 5″, no mark
Pitcher, 5½″, no mark, Artist Signed: L

Row 2:

Vase, 10″, no mark, Artist Signed: M
Lamp base, 11″, no mark
Vase, 9½″, no mark, Artist Signed: C
Vase, 8″, no mark, Artist Signed: C

MATT GREEN, before 1916

Bottom,
Left:

The gate, no mark

ANTIQUE MATT GREEN, before 1916

Bottom,
Right:

Vase, 9½″, no mark

* *Editors' Note* — Although matte with an e is now correct, the Roseville people always spelled it matt in their ads, catalogs and advertising material.

Plate 22

Plate 23

Plate 24

Plate 25

Plate 26

DUTCH, before 1916

Top,
Left:

Pitcher, 9½″, no mark
Mug, 5″, no mark, creamware with decal of Biblical scene.

Bottom,
Row 1:

Mug, 5″, no mark
Powder Box, 3″, no mark
Tobacco jar, 5″, no mark
Mug, 5″
Mug, 5″

Row 2:

Pitcher and Bowl, 9″, 12″ diameter, no mark
Pitcher, 11″
Tankard, 11½″

CREAMWARE

Top,
Right:

Chocolate pot, 10″, Cherry and Gold line Decal

Plate 27

Plate 28

Plate 29

STEIN SETS, before 1916

Top,
Left to Right:

Mug, 5″, Shrine emblem, Osman Temple, Feb. 14, 1916
Tankard, 11½″, Elk
Mug, 6½″, marked with the Rozane Ware Seal, Aladdin Patrol, Al. G. Field, Aug. 6 — 06.
Tankard, 11½″, Royal Order of Moose, "Howdy, Pap"
Mug, 5″, Same as above

ASH TRAYS AND MUG

Center,
Left to Right:

Ash Tray, "Drink Reyam Club Whiskey"
Mug, 5″, Creamware decorated by the pouncing technique
Ash Tray, "K. of P.", Grand Lodge, Zanesville, Ohio, June 8, 1915

DECORATED AND GOLD TRACED, before 1916

Bottom,
Left:

Candlestick, 9″, no mark

GOLD TRACED, before 1916

Bottom,
Right:

Candlestick, 9″, no mark

FORGET-ME-NOT, before 1916

Above,
Right:

Dresser Set, Creamware with decal, in light blue or lavender, no mark.

Plate 30

Plate 31

Plate 32

Plate 33

Plate 34

CARNELIAN, 1910-15,

marked with the large Rv, ink stamped Drip Glaze,
Top,
Left to Right,
Row 1:

Candleholder, 3″
Candleholder, 3″
Vase, 6″
Loving cup, 5″
Flower holder, 6″
Candleholder, 2½″

Row 2:

Urn, 8″
Ewer, 15″
Console Bowl, 14″

Heavy Textured Glaze,
also marked with large Rv (See page 28 for note.)

Bottom,
Left to Right:

Vase, 5″
Vase, 7″
Vase, 10″
Vase, 9″
Fan vase, 8″

Plate 35

Plate 36

MOSTIQUE, 1915

only occasionally found marked, large Rv stamp

Top,
Left to Right:

Vase, 6″
Vase, 10″
Large Jardiniere, 10″
Bowl, 2½″, beige glossy exterior
Vase, 6″

IMPERIAL I, 1924, no mark

Bottom,
Row 1:

Basket, 6″
Basket, 6″
Vase, 8″
Triple Bud Vase, 8″
Basket, 8″
Basket, 6″

Row 2:

Basket, 11″
Vase, 10″
Bud Vase, 12″
Basket, 13″

Plate 37

Plate 38

CERAMIC DESIGN, before 1916, no mark

Top
Left:

Powder Box, 4″
Wall Pocket
Wall Pocket

Bottom,
Right:

Planter with liner, 6½″ × 4″

MEDALLION, before 1916, no mark

Top,
left:

Dresser set, Tray 10″, Ring tree, Hair Receiver, Powder Box

EARLY PITCHERS, before 1916

Center,
Left to Right:

Landscape, 7½″
Tulips, 7½″

ROSEVILLE DEALER SIGNS

"Roseville Pottery" display sign, 4½″ × 10″
"Roseville" Display sign, 5″ × 8″
"Roseville" Display sign, 2″ × 6″

Plate 39: Ceramic Design

Plate 40

Plate 41

Plate 42

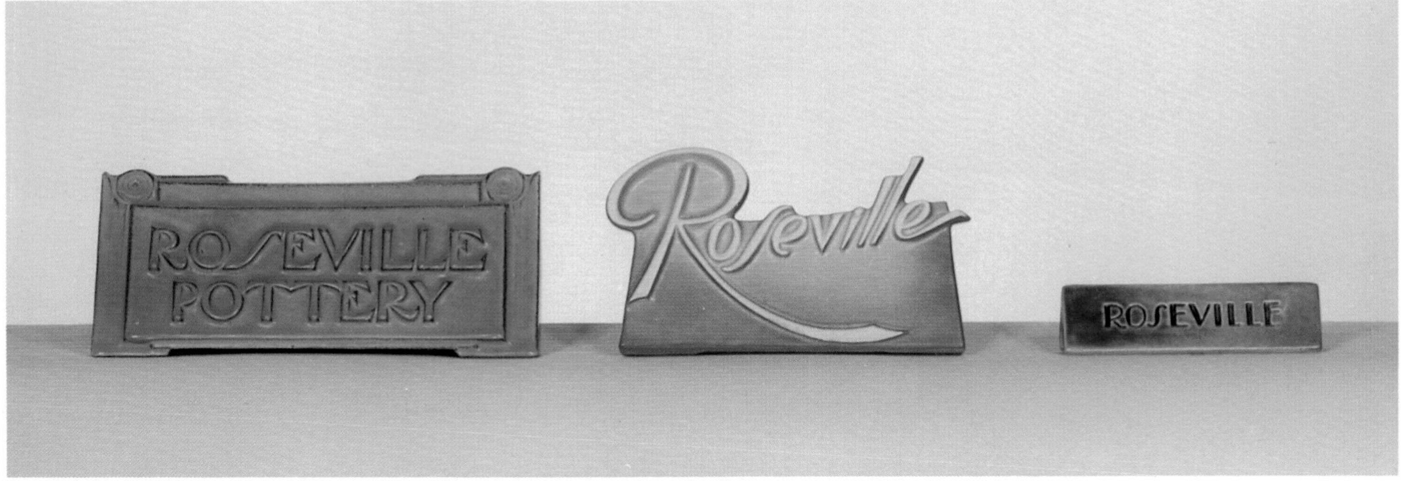

Plate 43

LANDSCAPE, 1910

Top,
Left to Right:

Covered sugar, 3½″, no mark
Planter, 4½″, no mark
Creamer, 3″, no mark

DECORATED UTILITY WARE, 1920

Marked with large Rv, ink stamp

Bottom,
Left to Right:

Pitcher, 7″
Pitcher, 6″
Pitcher, 7″
Pitcher, 4″

Plate 44

Plate 45

DONATELLO, 1915

Although much Donatello was not marked, occasionally it is marked with the large Rv ink stamp, or with the impressed Donatello, R P Co mark.

Row 1:
Left to Right:

Flower pot, and saucer, impressed Donatello mark, 5″
Compote, 4″, marked with the large Rv stamp
Large Bowl, 3½″
Bowl, 3″

Row 2:

Double Bud vase, 5″
Compote, 5″
Vase, 6″
Tall Candlestick, 8″
Vase, 8″

Row 3:

Pitcher, 6½″, marked with the Rv stamp
Vase, 10″, unusual grey and beige
Wall pocket, 10″
Jardiniere, 6″, marked with the Rv stamp

Row 4:

Basket, 15″
Jardiniere, 8½″
Frog
Jardiniere, 7″

Plate 46

JUVENILE, before 1916 — (?)

Matt glaze unless noted

Row 1:

Mug, 3″, standing rabbit, marked with small Rv stamp
Bowl, (under mug), 5½″
Two handled mug, 3″, high gloss, with sitting dog
"Baby's Plate", rolled edge, 6½″, with chicks
Oatmeal bowl, 5½″, with standing rabbit
Footed egg cup, 3″, with chick
Mug, 3½″, with chick

Row 2:

Plate, 7″, with chicks
Mug, 3″, with chicks
Plate, 8″, with standing rabbit, marked with small Rv stamp
Two handled mug, 3″, with standing rabbit
Rolled edge plate, 8″, high gloss, with ducks

Row 3:

Rolled edge plate, 8″, "Little Bo Peep", small Rv stamp
Creamer, 3½″, high gloss with Peter Rabbit, small Rv stamp
Rolled edge plate, 8″, "Tom The Piper's Son"
Creamer, 3½″, high gloss with Sunbonnet Girl, Rv stamp in gold
Rolled Edge Plate, 8″, "Little Jack Horner"

Bottom:

Milk pitcher, with chicks
Side pour creamer, with standing rabbit
Chamber, with chicks
Little pitcher, with saucer, both with chicks
Milk pitcher, with standing rabbit

Plate 47

Plate 48

ROZANE, 1917

Marked with the ROSEVILLE POTTERY, ROZANE, ink stamp in black, brown, or blue.

Top,
Right to Left,
Row 1:

Basket, 6″, in pink
Candlestick, 6″, in blue
Spittoon, 5″, in ivory
Compote, 5″, in green

Row 2:

Basket, 8″, in green
Basket, 11″, in ivory
Champagne bucket, in ivory
Vase, 7″, in yellow

VELMOSS SCHROLL, 1916

Bottom,
Left:

Jardiniere and Pedestal, 10″, jardiniere, 30″ overall

Bottom,
Right,
Row 1:

Candlestick, 8″
Bowl, 2½″ × 9″
Candlestick, 9″

Row 2:

Vase, 6″
Compote, 9″ diameter, 4″ high
Candlestick, 9″

Plate 49

Plate 50

Plate 51

ROSECRAFT, 1916-19

Marked with the Rv ink stamp

Top,
Left:

Vase, 8″

Top,
Right:

Vase, w/h, 6″
Bowl, 2½″
Frog

FLORANE, 1920's

Marked with the Rv ink stamp

Center,
Left to Right:

Bowl, 8″ diameter
Vase, 6″
Pair Bud vases, 8″
Urn vase, 3½″

ROSECRAFT BLACK, 1916

Center,
Right:

Vase, w/h, 10″, no mark

PERSIAN, 1916

Bottom,
Left to Right:

Sugar and creamer, no mark
Large Jardiniere, no mark
Bowl, 3½″, no mark

Plate 52

Plate 53

Plate 54

Plate 55

Plate 56

SAVONA, 1924-28

Top,
Left:

Vase, 10″, no mark

NORMANDY, 1924

Top,
Right:

Jardiniere, 7″, no mark

VICTORIAN ART POTTERY, 1924-28

Center,
Left to Right:

Covered jar, 8″, marked with the large Rv ink stamp
Urn, 10″, same mark as above

CORINTHIAN, 1923

Marked with the large Rv ink stamp
Bottom,
Left to Right,
Row 1:

Vase, 6″
Compote, 10″ diameter, 5″ high
Ash tray, 2″
Double bud vase, 7″

Row 2:

Candlestick, 8″
Vase, 8″
Vase, 10½″
Vase, 8″
Candlestick, 10″

Plate 57

Plate 58

Plate 59

Plate 60

DOGWOOD I, 1916-18

Top
Row,
Two Center
Items:

Wall pocket, marked with the small Rv ink stamp
Vase, 6″, marked with the large Rv ink stamp

DOGWOOD II, 1928, no mark

Row 1:

Basket, 6″, extreme left
Bowl, 2″, extreme right

Row 2:

Basket, 8″
Boat planter, 6″
Double wall pocket
Bud vase, 8″

Row 3:

Vase, 8″
Bud vase, 9″
Vase, 9″
Vase, 12″
Jardiniere, 8″

Plate 61

ROSECRAFT VINTAGE, 1924

Marked with the large Rv ink stamp

Row 1:

Vase, 5″
Bowl, 5″
Vase, 8″
Candlestick, 8″
Bowl, 6″ diameter

Row 2:

Jardiniere, 9″
Bowl, 3½″ diameter
Urn vase, 10″
Jardiniere, 8″

ROSECRAFT HEXAGON, 1924

Bottom,
Left to Right:

Vase, 6″, marked with the small Rv ink stamp
Bowl vase, 4″, marked with the small Rv ink stamp
Vase, 6″, same as above

Plate 62

Plate 63

PANEL, 1920

Marked with the RV ink stamp

Row 1:

Double bud vase,
Fan vase, 6″, with nude
Fan vase, 8″, with nude
Candleholder, 2″
Pillow vase, 6″

Row 2:

Candlestick, 8″
Urn vase, 8″
Vase, 9″
Vase, w/h, 8″
Candlestick, 8″

LA ROSE, 1924

Marked with the Rv ink stamp

Bottom,
Row 1:

Bowl, 6″ diameter
Bowl, 9″ diameter
Pr. Candleholders, 4″

Row 2:

Double bud vase
Pr vases, 10″
Double bud vase

Plate 64

Plate 65

DAHLROSE, 1924-28

Marked with black paper label

Row 1:

Triple bud vase, 6″
Square vase, 6″
Bowl, w/h, oval, 10″ across
Double bud vase

Row 2:

Vase, w/h, 8″
Square vase, 10″
Vase, w/h, 10″
Vase, w/h, 10"
Bud vase, 8″

TUSCANY, 1927

Bottom,
Left to Right:
Row 1:

Pair candleholders, 4″, no mark
Flower arranger-vase, 5″, no mark
Pair candleholders, 3″, no mark

Row 2:

Vase, 8″, no mark
Console bowl, 11″ across, no mark
Vase, 8″, no mark

Plate 66

Plate 67

FLORENTINE, 1924-28

Marked with the Rv ink stamp

Top,
Left to Right:

Double bud vase, 6″
Basket, 8″
Footed Compote, 10″ diameter
Vase, w/h, ivory, 9″
Lamp
Compote, ivory, 5″
Wall pocket, 7″
Vase, 8½″
Wall pocket, 9½″
Vase, 6½″
Bowl, 9″ diameter

LUSTRE, 1921

Center,
Left:

Candleholder, 8″, marked with large black paper label.
Candleholder, 10″, marked with black paper label
Vase, 10″, marked with large black paper label
Candleholder, 6″, marked with large black paper label

IMPERIAL II, 1924

Marked with black paper label

Bottom,
Right:

Vase, 6½″
Wall pocket

Plate 68

Plate 69

Plate 70

FUTURA, 1928
Marked with the black paper label

Top,
Left:
- Vase, 8″
- Vase, 8″

Top,
Right:
- Vase, 6″

Center,
Left to Right,
Row 1:
- Bud vase, 6″
- Candleholder, 4″
- Planter, 7″ across
- Candleholder, 4″
- Vase, 6″

Row 2:
- Vase, 8″, pink and grey high gloss
- Candlestick/bud vase, 10″
- Urn, 10″
- Vase with sea gulls, 10″
- Vase, w/h, 8″

CREMONA, 1927
Occasionally marked with black paper label

Bottom,
Left:
- Vase, w/h, 10″

Bottom,
Right,
Row 1:
- Candleholder, 4″
- Vase, 7″
- Candleholder, 4″

Row 2:
- Vase, 10½″
- Frog
- Bowl, 9″ across
- Vase, 8″

"The criterion of true beauty is, that it increases on examination." —GREVILLE

A FEW art objects, discreetly placed, add so much to a home! Not the hit-and-miss massing of Victorian days, but the tasteful arrangement of 1928.

And just here it is that Roseville serves so incomparably! Charming Roseville Pottery, created with that touch of genius by men and women who love their craft.

Beauty that grows as you live with it, such is the essence of Roseville Pottery. For instance, the jar and vases pictured here. Adorable they are, in delicate tints, daintily decorated with arrowheads.

These pieces and a diversity of other designs . . . bowls, jars, vases, candlesticks in a wide selection of sizes, shapes and colors . . . can be seen at good stores. For the home or as gifts they have a distinction of their own.

You will want a copy of the interesting booklet, "Pottery." Write for it.

THE ROSEVILLE POTTERY CO., *Zanesville, Ohio*

ROSEVILLE POTTERY

Plate 71

Plate 72

Plate 73

Plate 74

Plate 75

EARLAM, 1930

Top,
Left,
Row 1:

Pair Candleholders, 6″
Wall hanging crocus pot

Row 2:

Urn, 6″, silver paper sticker
Urn, w/h, 6″

IXIA, 1930's

Mark: Impressed Roseville

Top,
Right,
Row 1:

Basket, 10″, Shape No. 346
Vase, 6″, Shape No. 853

Row 2:

Bowl, 4, Shape No. 326
Bowl, 6″, Shape No. 387

CLEMANA, 1934

Bottom,
Left,
Row 1:

Vase, 7″, no mark

Row 2:

Pair Candleholders, 4½″, no mark

SUNFLOWER, 1930

Marked with the black paper label

Row 1:

Urn, 5½″
Vase, 8″
Vase, 7″
Vase, 6″

Row 2:

Vase, 10″
Jardiniere, 9″
Vase, 8″

Plate 76

Plate 77

Plate 78

Plate 79

THORN APPLE, 1930's
Mark: Impressed Roseville

Top,
Left,
Row 1:
Cornucopia vase, 6″
Planter, 5″, Shape No. 262
Vase, w/h, 6″, Shape No. 812
Row 2:
Pair Candleholders, 2½″, Shape No. 1117
Candleholder, 5½″
Row 3:
Vase, 4″, Shape No. 308
Basket, 10″, Shape No. 342

IRIS, 1938

Top,
Right,
Row 1:
Bowl vase, 4″, Shape No. 2117, Roseville impressed
Wall shelf, 8″, Roseville impressed
Bowl, w/h, 5″, Shape No. 359, Roseville impressed
Row 2:
Vase, 4″, Shape No. 914, Roseville, in relief
Planter, 14″, Shape No. 364, Roseville impressed
Candleholder, 4″, Shape No. 1135, Roseville impressed
Row 3:
Ewer, 10″, Shape No. 926, Roseville impressed
Basket, 8″, Shape No. 354, Roseville impressed

POPPY, 1930's
Mark: Impressed Roseville

Bottom,
Left,
Row 1:
Wall Pocket, Candleholder, 9″
Shape No. 1281
Vase, 6½″
Row 2:
Ewer, 10″, Shape No. 876
Basket, 10″, Shape No. 347

MOSS, 1930's
Mark: Impressed Roseville

Bottom,
Right,
Row 1:
Pair Candleholders, 4½″
Shape No. 1107
Row 2:
Vase, 6″, Shape No. 774
Urn, 8″, Shape No. 774
Row 3:
Console, 13″

Plate 80

Plate 81

Plate 82

Plate 83

A free copy of the illustrated booklet, "Pottery", will be gladly sent on request.

Gifts of pottery inspire delight at your thoughtfulness and the good taste of your choice.

Particularly fascinating are the new Roseville creations. Charm of contour and beauty of color impel one to choose these bowls, jars, vases and candlesticks. And the loving craftsmanship with which they are fashioned captures, as surely as the holiday season comes, the heart of the recipient.

There is an entrancing variety of sizes, shapes and designs in Roseville Pottery . . . and the prices are so modest! Ask to see the Roseville displays at leading gift shops and department stores.

THE ROSEVILLE POTTERY COMPANY
ZANESVILLE, OHIO

ROSEVILLE POTTERY

FERELLA, 1931

Top,
Left to Right:

Vase, 4″
Vase, 9″
Bowl, 12″
Vase, 6″
Vase, 9″

FALLINE, 1933

Marked with silver paper label

Center,
Left to Right:

Vase, 6″
Urn vase, 8″
Lamp
Vase, 7″
Vase, 6″

TOURMALINE, 1933

Marked with silver or gold paper label

Bottom,
Left:

Ginger jar

Bottom,
Right:
Row 1:

Bowl vase, 5″
Vase, 8″
Frog

Row 2:

Vase, 6″
Planter, 5 × 12½″
Vase, 6″

Plate 84

Plate 85

Plate 86

Plate 87

MONTICELLO, 1931

Top,
Left,
Row 1:
Vase, 4″
Basket, 6½″
Vase, 4″
Row 2:
Pair of Vases, extreme right and left, 6″
Vase, center, 7″
Row 3:
Pair of vases, extreme right and left, 7″
Urn, 9″

WINDSOR, 1931

Mark: Black or silver paper sticker

Top,
Right,
Row 1:
Pair candlesticks, extreme right and left, 4½″
vase, 5″
Row 2:
Vase, 5″
Console/planter, 16″ across, frog
Row 3:
Vase, 7″
Vase, 9″
Vase, 7″

COSMOS, 1940

Mark: Roseville impressed or in relief

Bottom,
Left,
Row 1:
Vase, 4″, Shape No. 954
Bowl, 6″, Shape No. 376
Vase, 3″
Row 2:
Basket, 12″
Candleholder, 2½″
Ewer, 15″, Shape No. 951

JONQUIL, 1931

Row 1:
Bowl, 4″
Basket, 9″
Bud vase, 7″
Bowl, 4″
Row 2:
Vase, 8″
Basket, 10″
Bowl, 5½″

Plate 88

Plate 89

Plate 90

Plate 91

BLACKBERRY, 1933

Mark: Black paper label

Row 1:

Jug, 5″
Vase, 4″
Vase, 6″
Wall pocket,
Bowl, 8″ across

Row 2:

Urn vase, 6″
Jardiniere, 6″
Vase, 6″
Vase, 5″

Row 3:

Pair candleholders, 4½″
Console bowl, 13″ across
Vase, 4″

Row 4:

Vase, 8″
Vase, 10″
Vase, 12½″
Vase, 8″

Plate 92

CHERRY BLOSSOM, 1933

Mark: Silver or gold paper label
or Large silver paper label

Row 1:

Pair candleholders, 4″
Bowl, 6″
Bowl, 5″

Row 2:

Vase, 5″
Vase, 7½″
Vase, 10″
Jug vase, 7″

Row 3:

Vase, 5″
Vase, 7″
Vase, 8″
Jug vase, 7″
Jug vase, 4″

Row 4:

Lamp base
Jardiniere, 10″
Urn vase, 8″

Plate 93

BANEDA, 1933

Mark: Black paper label

Top,
Row 1:

Vase, 5½″
Candleholder, 4½″
Console, 13″ across
Candleholder, 4½″
Vase, 6″

Row 2:

Vase, 8″
Large jardiniere, 9½″
Vase, 8″

WISTERIA, 1933

Mark: Large and small silver sticker

Bottom,
Row 1:

Console bowl, 12″
Vase, 7″
Vase, 6″
Bowl, 4″

Row 2:

Vase, 8″
Vase, 9″
Vase, 10″
Urn, 7½″

Plate 94

Plate 95

LAUREL, 1934
Mark: Silver paper sticker

Top,
Row 1:

Bowl, 7″ across
Vase, 7″
Vase, 6½″
Vase, 6″

Row 2:

Vase, 8″
Vase, 9″
Vase, 8½″
Vase, 6″

LUFFA, 1934
Mark: Gold paper label

Bottom,
Left to Right:

Bowl, 4″
Vase, 7″
Vase, 13″
Vase, 7″
Vase, 6″

Plate 96

Plate 97

TOPEO, 1934

Mark: Silver or gold paper label

Top,
Left:

Vase, 9½″

Note: Some feel the Red-Glazed Topeo should be properly identified as Mowa. Nothing in our resear[illegible] can confirm nor deny this.

Center,
Left:

Vase, 7″
Vase, 9″

Top,
Right,
Row 1:

Bowl, 2½″

Row 2:

Urn, 6″
Vase, 6½″

PRIMROSE, 1932

Mark: Roseville impressed

Bottom,
Left to Right:

Vase, 8″, Shape No. 767
Bowl, 4″
Vase, 8″, Shape No. 765

Plate 98

Plate 99

Plate 100

Plate 101

PINECONE, 1931

Marks: Roseville impressed or in relief,
Black paper label
or PINE CONE impressed

Row 1:

Triple candleholders, 5½″, Shape No. 1106
Bowl, 3″, Shape No. 632
Planter, 3½″, Shape No. 468
Planter, 6″, Shape No. 456
Basket, 6″, Shape No. 408

Row 2:

Fan Vase, 6″, Shape No. 472
Console Bowl, 15″ across, Shape No. 323
Cornucopia, 8″, Shape No. 128

Row 3:

Ice lip pitcher, 8″
Cornucopia, 6″, Shape No. 126
Boat-basket, 10″, Shape No. 410
Pitcher, 9″, Shape No. 415

Row 4:

Vase, 10″, Shape No. 109
Basket, 9″ × 13″, Shape No. 339
Vase, 7″, Shape No. 478
Basket, 10″, Shape No. 338

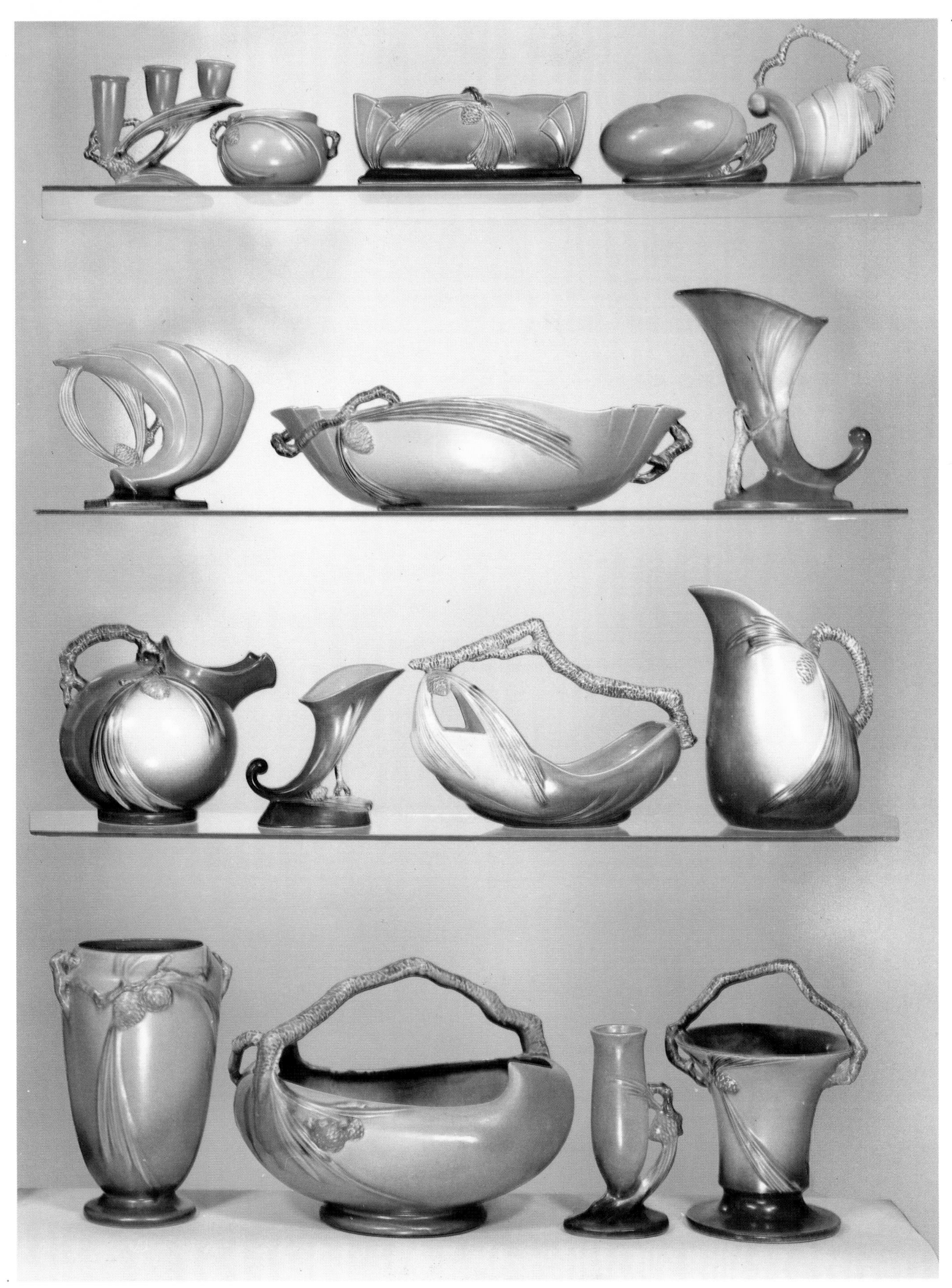

Plate 102

ORIAN, 1935
Mark: Gold paper label

Top,
Left to Right:

Vase, 7″
Vase, 8″
Vase, 12″
Bowl 6″

RUSSCO, 1930's
Mark: Gold paper label

Center,
Left:

Vase, 14½″
Vase, 6½″

Center,
Right:

Bud vase, 8″
Vase, 6″

VELMOSS, II, 1935
Mark: Gold paper label

Bottom,
Left to Right:

Vase, 7″
Double Bud 8″
Vase, 6″

Bottom,
Far Right:

Double Cornucopia, 8½″

Plate 103

Plate 104

Plate 105

Plate 106

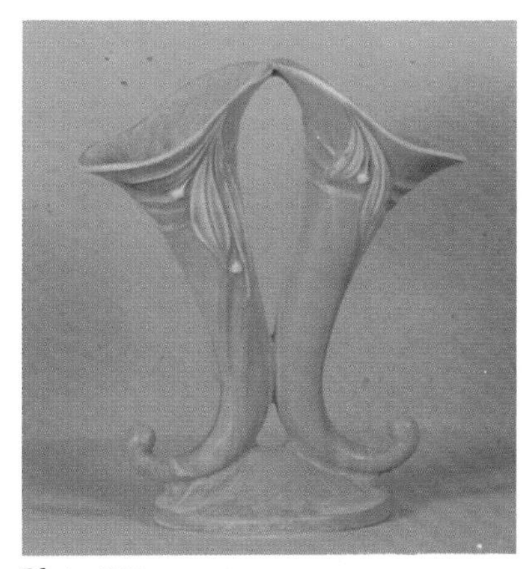
Plate 107

MORNING GLORY, 1935

Mark: Gold paper label

Top,
Row 1:

Bowl vase, 4″
Urn vase, 6″
Vase, 7″
Vase, 6″

Row 2:

Vase, 8″
Vase, 12″
Vase, 10″

TEASEL, 1936

Mark: Roseville impressed, or silver paper label

Center,

Row 1:

Vase, w/h, 5″
Vase, 6″, Shape No. 348
Vase, 6″, Shape No. 882
Bowl, 4″, Shape No. 342

Row 2:

Basket, 10″, Shape No. 349
Ewer, 18″, Shape No. 890
Basket, 10″, Shape No. 349

DAWN, 1937

Mark: Impressed Roseville

Bottom,
Left:

Vase, 6″, Shape No. 827
Vase, 8″, Shape No. 828
Vase, 6″, Shape No. 826

MODERNE, 1930's

Mark: Roseville impressed, or silver paper label

Bottom,
Right:

Lamp, 9″, Shape No. 799
Vase, 7″, Shape No. 794

Plate 108

Plate 109

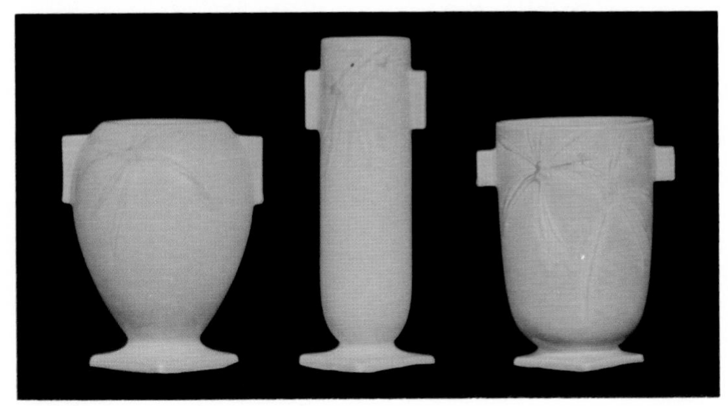

Plate 110

Plate 111

FUSCHIA, 1939

Mark: Roseville impressed

Top,
Left,
Row 1:

Ice lip pitcher, 8″, Shape No. 1322

Row 2:

Bowl, 4″, Shape No. 346
Bowl vase, 3″, Shape No. 645

Row 3:

Vase, 7″, Shape No. 895
Vase, 12″, Shape No. 903
Basket and frog, 8″, Shape No. 350

IVORY II, 1937

Mark: Roseville impressed, or silver paper label

Top,
Center:

Vase, w/h, 10″, Carnelian shape

Top,
Right:

Vase, 6″, Savona shape

Center,
Right,
Row 1:

Bowl vase, 6″, Russco shape, Shape No. 259

Row 2:

Candelabra, 5½″ high, Velmoss II shape, Shape No. 1116
Bowl, w/h, 6″ diameter, Matt Color shape, Shape No. 550

BLEEDING HEART, 1938

Mark: Roseville in relief

Bottom,
Row 1:

Vase, 4″, Shape No. 138
Wall Pocket, 8″, Shape No. 1287
Pitcher, Shape No. 1323
Ewer, 6″, Shape No. 963

Row 2:

Basket, 10″, Shape No. 360
Basket, 12″, Shape No. 361
Ewer, 10″, Shape No. 972

Plate 112

Plate 113

Plate 114

Plate 115

Plate 116

ROZANE PATTERN, 1940's
Mark: Roseville in relief

Top,
Left:

Bud vase, 6", Shape No. 2
Planter, 14", Shape No. 397
Vase, w/h, 6", Shape No. 398

GARDENIA, 1940's
Mark: Roseville in relief

Top,
Right,
Row 1:

Bowl 4", Shape No. 600

Row 2:

Cornucopia, 6", Shape No. 621
Basket, 8", Shape No. 608
Ewer, 6", Shape No. 616

Row 3:

Ewer, 10", Shape No. 617
Basket, 10", Shape No. 609
Double Cornucopia, 8", Shape No. 622

BITTERSWEET, 1940
Mark: Roseville in relief

Bottom,
Row 1:

Double Bud vase, 6", Shape No. 873
Basket, 10", Shape No. 810
Vase, 5", Shape No. 972

Row 2:

Planter, 8" long, Shape No. 868
Tea set,
Tea Pot, Shape No. 871P
Sugar, Shape No. 871S
Creamer, Shape No. 871C

Row 3:

Basket, 6", Shape No. 808
Basket, 8", Shape No. 809
Vase, 8", Shape No. 883
Cornucopia, 8", Shape No. 882
Ewer, 8", Shape No. 816

Plate 117

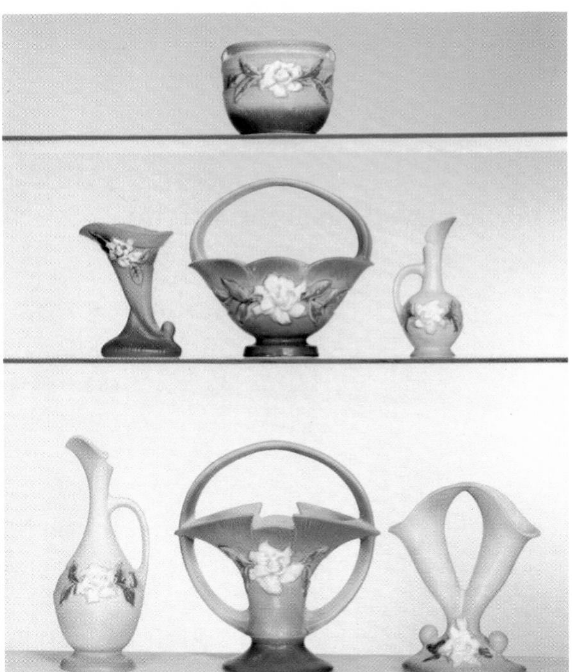

Plate 118

Plate 119

WHITE ROSE, 1940's

Mark: Roseville in relief

Row 1:

Frog, w/h, Shape No. 41
Cornucopia, 6″, Shape No. 143
Bowl, w/h, 4″, Shape No. 387
Bowl, w/h, 3″, Shape No. 653

Row 2:

Cornucopia, 8″, Shape No. 144
Basket, 10″, Shape No. 363
Bowl, w/h, 4″, Shape No. 653
Ewer, 10″, Shape No. 990

Row 3:

Double cornucopia, 8″, Shape No. 145
Tea Set,
Tea Pot, Shape No. 1-T
Sugar, Shape No. 1-S
Creamer, Shape No. 1-C
Urn vase, 8″, Shape No. 147

Row 4:

Basket, 12″, Shape No. 364
Ewer, 15″, Shape No. 993
Ewer, 6″, Shape No. 981
Pitcher, Shape No. 1324

Plate 120

WATER LILY, 1940's

Mark: Roseville in relief

Row 1:

Bowl, 3″, Shape No. 663
Ewer, 6″, Shape No. 10
Vase, 6″, Shape No. 73
Cornucopia, 6″, Shape No. 177

Row 2:

Ewer, 10″, Shape No. 11
Cookie Jar, 10″, Shape No. 1
Basket, 10″, Shape No. 381
Vase, 10″, Shape No. 81

Row 3:

Vase, 7″, Shape No. 75
Cornucopia, 8″, Shape No. 178
Vase, 6″, Shape No. 72
Basket, 8″, Shape No. 380

Row 4:

Vase, 12″, Shape No. 81
Basket, 12″, Shape No. 382
Ewer, 15″, Shape No. 12

Plate 121

ZEPHYR LILY, 1940's
Mark: Roseville in relief

Row 1:

Bowl, w/h 4″, Shape No. 671
Console boat, 10″, Shape No. 475
Bowl, w/h 8″, Shape No. 474

Row 2:

Basket, 7″, Shape No. 393
Cookie Jar, 10″, Shape No. 5
Ash tray
Vase, 10″, Shape No. 138

Row 3:

Basket, 8″, Shape No. 394
Tea Set, (Tea pot, Sugar and Creamer) Shape No. 7
Cornucopia, 6″, Shape No. 203

Row 4:

Basket, 10″, Shape No. 395
Vase, w/h, 7″, Shape No. 131
Ewer, 15″, Shape No. 24
Ewer, 10″, Shape No. 23
Vase, 10″, Shape No. 137

Plate 122

PEONY, 1930's

Mark: Roseville in relief

Row 1:

Bowl, w/h, 4″, Shape No. 427
Vase, w/h, 6″, Shape No. 168
Bowl, w/h, 4″, Shape No. 427

Row 2:

Double Cornucopia, Shape No. 172
Basket, 10″, Shape No. 378
Basket, 7″, Shape No. 376

Row 3:

Ewer, 6″, Shape No. 7
Tea Set, (Tea Pot, Sugar and Creamer,) Shape No. 3
Bowl, w/h, 4″, Shape No. 661

Row 4:

Vase, w/h, 4″, Shape No. 57
Ewer, 10″, Shape No. 8
Ewer, 10″, Shape No. 8
Wall Pocket, 8″, Shape No. 1293

Plate 123

MAGNOLIA, 1940's
Mark: Roseville in relief

Row 1:

Planter, 8″ across, Shape No. 389
Double bud vase, 4½″, Shape No. 186
Vase, w/h, 4″, Shape No. 86
Bowl, w/h 3″, Shape No. 665

Row 2:

Ewer, 6″, Shape No. 13
Mug, 3″, Shape No. 3
Cider Pitcher, 7″, Shape No. 132
Mug, 3″, Shape No. 3
Basket, 8″, Shape No. 384 *

Row 3:

Basket, 7″, Shape No. 384 *
Tea Set, (Pot, sugar and creamer,) Shape No. 4

Row 4:

Basket, 10″, Shape No. 385
Ewer, 15″, Shape No. 15
Cookie Jar, 10″, Shape No. 2

**Note* Occasionally, as in this case, the same shape number will be found on two different shapes, within the same line.

Plate 124

COLUMBINE, 1940's.

Mark: Roseville in relief

Top,
Row 1:

Ewer, 7″, Shape No. 18
Bowl, w/h, 6″, Shape No. 401
Basket, 7″, Shape No. 365
Ewer, 7″, Shape No. 18

Row 2:

Basket, 10″, Shape No. 367
Bowl, w/h, 3″, Shape No. 655
Basket, 12″, Shape No. 368
Vase, w/h, 8″, Shape No. 20

FOXGLOVE, 1940's

Mark: Roseville in relief

Bottom,
Row 1:

Vase, w/h, 4″, Shape No. 42
Vase, w/h, 3″, Shape No. 659
Basket, 8″, Shape No. 373
Conch Shell, 6″, Shape No. 426
Double bud vase, 4½″, Shape No. 160

Row 2:

Ewer, 6½″, Shape No. 4
Cornucopia, 8″, Shape No. 164
Candleholder, 4½″, Shape No. 1150
Ewer, 15″, Shape No. 6
Ewer, 10″, Shape No. 5

Plate 125

Plate 126

FREESIA, 1945

Mark: Roseville in relief

Row 1:

Ewer, 6″, Shape No. 19
Flower Pot, 5″, Shape No. 670
Bookends, pair, Shape No. 15

Row 2:

Basket, 8″, Shape No. 391
Pitcher, 10″, Shape No. 20
Basket, 10″, Shape No. 392
Cornucopia, 8″, Shape No. 198

Row 3:

Vase, w/h, 8″, Shape No. 122
Tea Set, (Pot, sugar and creamer) Shape No. 6
Vase, w/h 7″, Shape No. 120

Row 4:

Cookie jar, 10″, Shape No. 4
Ewer, 15″, Shape No. 21
Urn, w/h, 8″, Shape 196
Candleholder, w/h, 4½″, Shape No. 1161
Bud vase, w/h, 7″, Shape No. 195

Plate 127

CLEMATIS, 1944

Mark: Roseville in relief

Row 1:

Bowl, w/h, 4″, Shape No. 445
Double bud vase, 5″, Shape No. 194
Cornucopia, 6″, Shape No. 140
Candleholder, w/h, 4½″, Shape No. 11

Row 2:

Basket, 8″, Shape No. 388
Bud vase, w/h, 7″, Shape No. 187
Ewer, 10″, Shape No. 17
Basket, 7″, Shape No. 387
Ewer, 6″, Shape No. 16

Row 3:

Vase, w/h, 8″, Shape No. 108
Tea Set, (Pot, sugar and creamer) Shape No. 5
Vase, w/h, 6″, Shape No. 188

Row 4:

Cookie jar, 10″, Shape No. 3
Wall Pocket, 8″, Shape No. 1295
Ewer, 15″, Shape No. 18
Basket, 10″, Shape No. 389

Plate 128

APPLE BLOSSOM, 1948

Mark: Roseville in relief

Row 1:

Cornucopia, 6″, Shape No. 381*
Hanging Basket
Vase, w/h, 6″, Shape No. 381*

Row 2:

Tea Set, (Pot, sugar and creamer), Shape No. 371
Basket, 8″, Shape No. 309

Row 3:

Ewer, 8″, Shape No. 316
Vase, w/h, 7″, Shape No. 382
Basket, 10″, Shape No. 310
Bud vase, w/h, 7″, Shape No. 379

Row 4:

Vase, w/h, 9″, Shape 387
Ewer, 15″, Shape No. 318
Basket, 12″, Shape No. 311

Plate 129

BUSHBERRY, 1948

Mark: Roseville in relief

Row 1:

Bowl, w/h, 4″, Shape No. 411
Basket, 6½″, Shape No. 369
Cornucopia, 6″, Shape No. 153
Vase, w/h, 6″, Shape No. 29
Bowl, 3″, Shape No. 657

Row 2:

Ewer, 6″, Shape No. 1
Cornucopia, Shape No. 3
Wall Pocket, 8″, Shape No. 1291
Basket, 8″, Shape No. 370

Row 3:

Tea Set, (Pot, sugar and creamer) Shape No. 2

Row 4:

Ewer, 10″, Shape No. 2
Basket, 12″, Shape No. 372
Cornucopia, 8″, Shape No. 154

Plate 130

SNOWBERRY, 1946

Mark: Roseville in relief

Row 1:

Ash tray
Console bowl, w/h, 10″ across, Shape No. 1BL1
Ewer, 6″, Shape No. 1TK

Row 2:

Basket, 7″, Shape No. 1BK
Cornucopia, 6″, Shape No. 1CC
Basket, 8″, Shape No. 1BK
Bowl, w/h, 5″, Shape No. 1RB

Row 3:

Ewer, 6″, Shape No. 1TK
Tea Set, (Pot, sugar and creamer) Shape Nos LTP, 1S, 1C
Bud vase, 7″, Shape No. 1BV

Row 4:

Basket, 8″, Shape No. 1BK
Ewer, 10″, Shape No. 1TK
Pair candleholders, Shape No. 1CS-1
Basket, 10″, Shape No. 1BK

Plate 131

MOCK ORANGE, 1950

Mark: Roseville, U. S. A., Mock Orange
in relief

Top,
Left,
Row 1:

Bowl, 4", Shape No. 900
Basket, 6", Shape No. 908
Ewer, 6", Shape No. 916

Row 2:

Tall square planter

Row 3:

Pair baskets, 8", Shape No. 909, marked U.S.A.

MING TREE, 1947

Top,
Right,
Row 1:

Pair candleholders, extreme left and right, Shape No. 551
Basket, 8", Shape No. 508

Row 2:

Console bowl, w/h, 10" across, Shape No. 528

Row 3:

Vase, w/h, 8", Shape No. 582
Ewer, 10", Shape No. 516
Vase, w/h, 6", Shape No. 581

MAYFAIR, late 40's

Mark: Roseville in relief

Center,
Left to Right:

Bowl, 4", Shape No. 1110
Pitcher, 8", Shape No. 1105
Tankard, 12", Shape No. 1107
Planter, 8", Shape No. 1113

BURMESE, 1950's

Bottom,
Left: Pair candleholder-bookends, extreme left and right,
White, Shape No. 80-B, Black Shape No. 70-B
Candlestick in center, Shape No. 75-B

ROYAL CAPRI, late line

Mark: Roseville in relief

Bottom,
Right:

Occasional piece

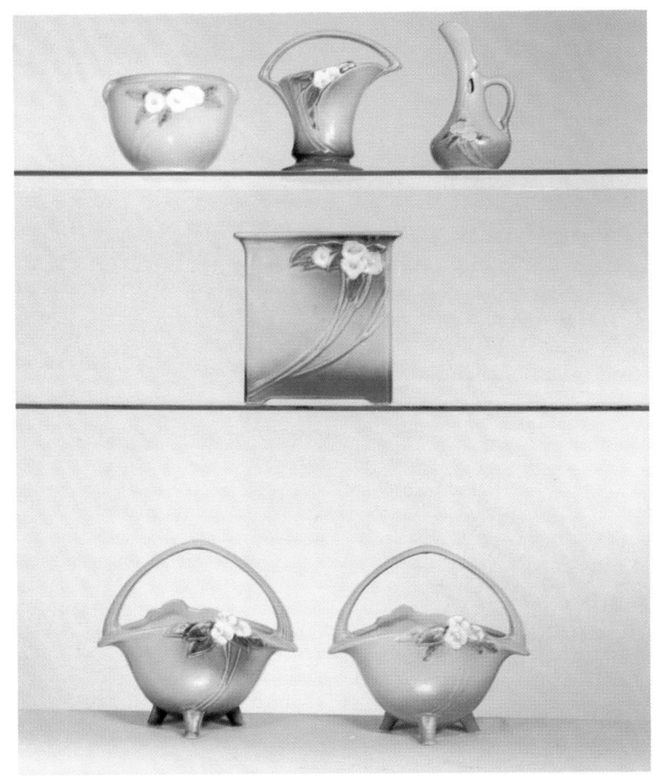
Plate 132

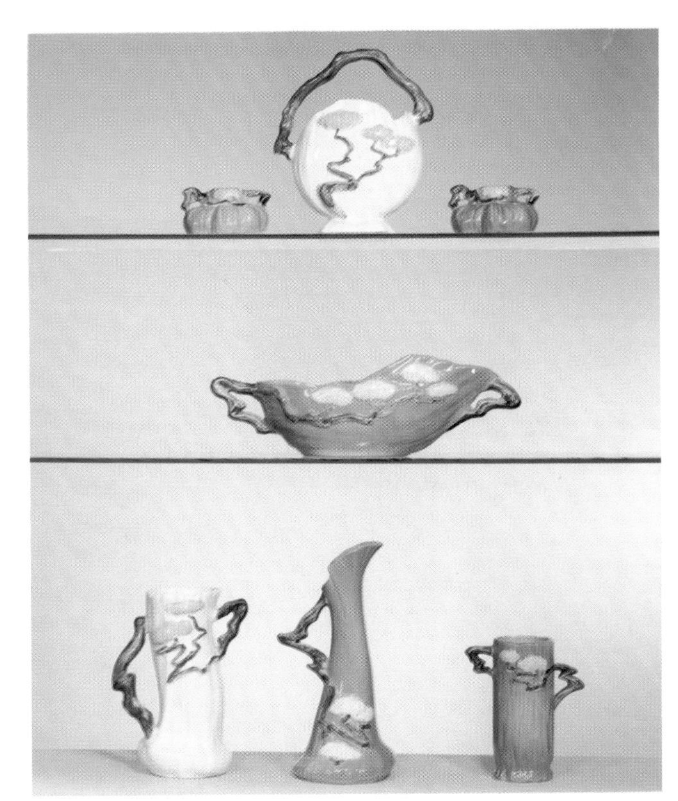
Plate 133

Plate 134

Plate 135

Plate 136

LOTUS, 1952

Mark: Lotus in relief

Top,
Left:

Pair candleholders, 2½", Shape No. L5
Vase, 10", Shape No. L3

PASADENA, 1952

Mark: Roseville, Pasadena Planter in relief

Top,
Right:

Occasional piece, 7", Shape No. 526
Pair flower pots, 4", Shape No. L36, (items 2 and 4)
Bowl, 3", Shape No. L24

UNNAMED LINE

Mark: Roseville in relief

Center,
Row 1:

Vase, w/h, 9", Shape No. 582
Occasional piece, 15", Shape No. 532
Boat-shape dish, 7", Shape No. 555

Row 2:

Conch shell, 7½", Glossy line, Shape No. 563
Shell
Bowl, 9", Shape No. 529
Tea Pot, Glossy line, Shape No. 14-P

COMMERCIAL LINE, 1940's

Mark: R, U S A in relief

Bottom,
Left to Right:

Vase, 6", Shape No. 80
Vase, 7", Shape No. 81
Vase, 9", Shape No. 82
Bowl, 9", Shape No. 61

Plate 137

Plate 138

Plate 139

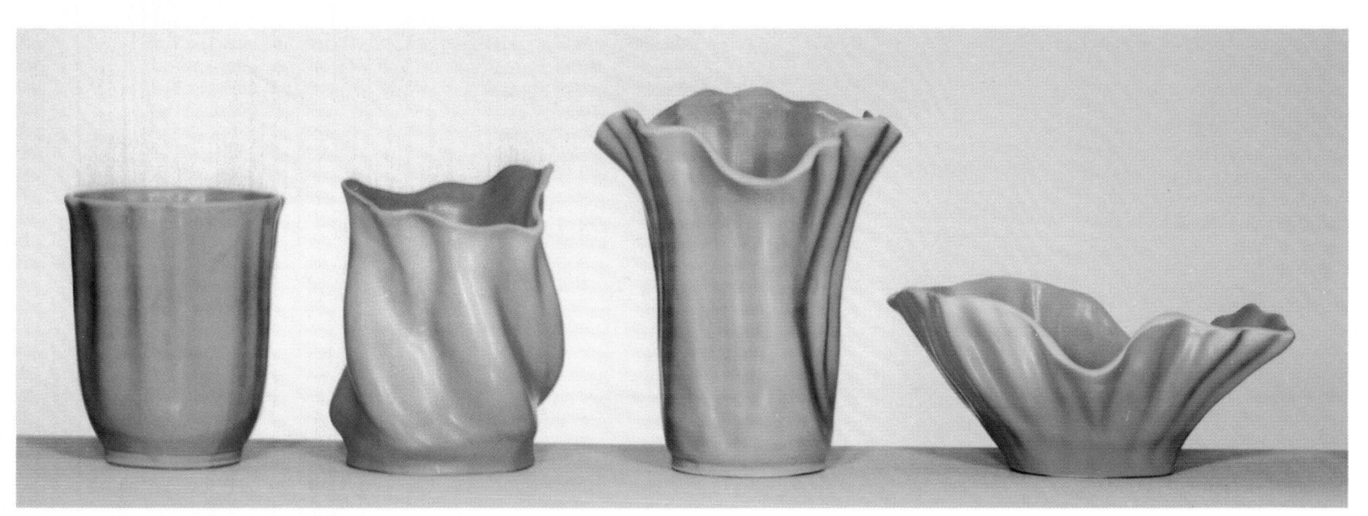
Plate 140

SILHOUETTE, 1952

Mark: Roseville in relief

Row 1:

Pair Candleholders, extreme left and right, 3″, Shape No. 751
Planter, 14″ long, center, Shape No. 731

Row 2:

Planter vase, 5″, Shape No. 756
Ewer, 6″, Shape No. 716
Ewer, 10″, Shape No. 717
Basket, 6″, Shape No. 708
Vase, 7″, Shape No. 782

Row 3:

Cornucopia, 8″, Shape No. 721
Fan vase, 7″, Shape No. 783
Ash tray, Shape No. 799
Basket, 8″, Shape No. 709

Row 4:

Basket, 10″, Shape No. 710
Cigarette box
Urn, 8″, Shape No. 763
Vase, 9″, Shape No. 785
Wall Pocket, 8″, Shape No. 766

Plate 141

WINCRAFT, 1948

Mark: Roseville in relief

Row 1:

Planter set, 6″, Shape Nos. 1051 and 1050
Tea set, (pot, sugar and creamer) Shape No. 271

Row 2:

Basket, 12″, Shape No. 209
Candleholders, pair, Shape No. 2CS
Circle vase, 8″, Shape No. 1053
Ewer, 8″, Shape No. 216

Row 3:

Planter, 10″, Shape No. 231
Cornucopia, 8″, Shape No. 222
Ewer, 6″, Shape No. 217
Basket, 8″, Shape No. 208

Row 4:

Vase, 8″, Shape No. 282
Vase, 10″, Shape No. 284
Vase, 10″, Shape No. 290
Vase, 10″, Shape No. 285
Vase, 6″, Shape No. 272

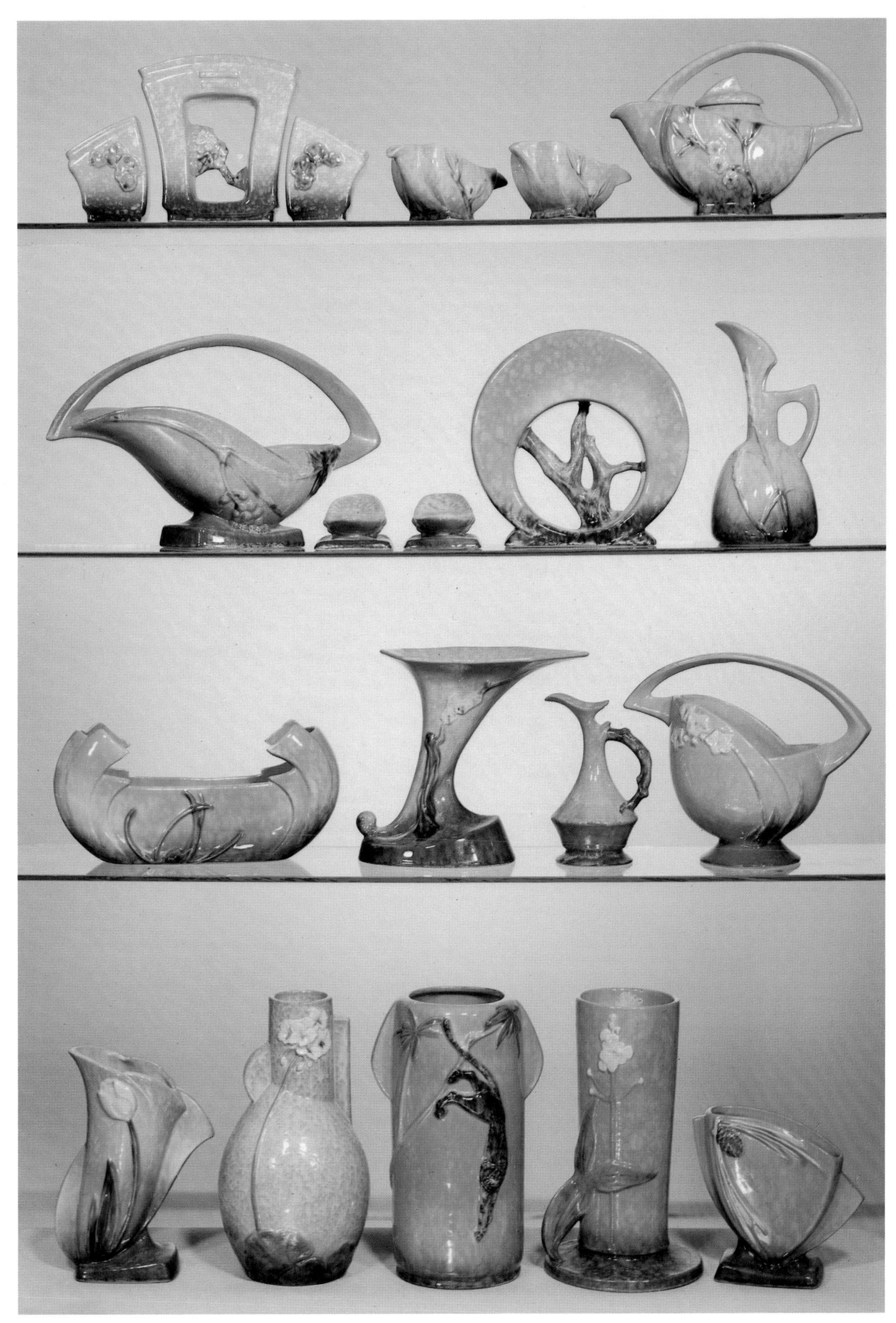

Plate 142

ELSIE, THE COW

Mark: The Borden Co., R. V. in relief

Top,
Left:

Mug, Shape No. B1
Plate, 7½", Shape No. B2
Bowl, Shape No. B3

RAYMOR, 1952

Mark: Raymor by Roseville, U.S.A. in relief

Top,
Right:

Bean pot, Shape No. 195
Swinging coffee pot, Shape No. 176
Bean Pot, Shape No. 194

Bottom,
Row 1:

Hot Plate, Shape No. 84-198 and casserole, Shape No. 198
Hot plate, Shape No. 159
Cup and Saucer, Shape No. 151

Row 2: Tea Set (pot, sugar and creamer) Sugar Shape No. 157
Creamer, Shape No. 158

Row 3:

Salad Plate, Shape No. 154
Dinner plate, Shape No. 152
Luncheon plate, Shape No. 153

Plate 143

Plate 144

Plate 145

JARDINIERES AND PEDESTALS, UMBRELLA STANDS

Top,
Left to Right:

Blackberry, Jardiniere and pedestal, 1933
Donatello, jardiniere and pedestal, 1915
Pine Cone, jardiniere and pedestal, 1931
Magnolia, jardiniere and pedestal, 1940

Bottom,
Left to Right:

Mostique, umbrella stand, 1915
Mostique, jardiniere and pedestal, 1915
Fuschia, jardiniere and pedestal, 1939
Freesia, jardiniere and pedestal, 1945

Jardinieres and pedestals were made in at least 42 of the Roseville patterns, as late as Bushberry in 1948. Some lines offered two sizes.

Plate 146

Plate 147

UMBRELLA STANDS AND SAND JARS

Top,
Left to Right:

Imperial I, Umbrella stand, 1916
Florentine, Umbrella stand, 1924-28
Pine Cone, Umbrella stand, 1931
Florentine II, sand jar, after 1937, marked Roseville in relief

UNIDENTIFIED

No matter how adept one may be at identifying pottery as to pattern, there always seems to be a few pieces difficult to categorize. So is the case with the photographs on the bottom half of the following page.

Bottom,
Left:

Lamp, marked with silver paper label

Bottom,
Right:

Vase, 8″, Shape No. 796, marked Roseville impressed
Square vase, with feet, marked with silver paper label
Vase, 8″, Shape No. 942, marked Roseville impressed

While the first vase would appear to be Moderne, the colors are certainly not standard. Several groupings of numbers appearing on the bottom of the vase, would indiciate that it was possibly an experimental item. As for the vase on the right, this pattern is shown in the Roseville catalogues only in the second Ivory line, but in such a number that it certainly must be one of the earlier lines whose shapes were used with the matte white glaze of second ivory. Perhaps one of our readers will be able to identify the line.

Bottom,
Center

Basket, 10″, Shape No. C-1012
(Does C stand for Crystal Green, as B stands for Burmese?)

Bottom,
Upper Right:

Basket, 8″, marked with the silver paper label. (Note similarity to handle of Rozane basket (1917). Smaller basket has been found with the tall pointed handle of the Jonquil basket. Some collectors feel this may be the Forrest line.)

Plate 148

Plate 149

Plate 150

Plate 151

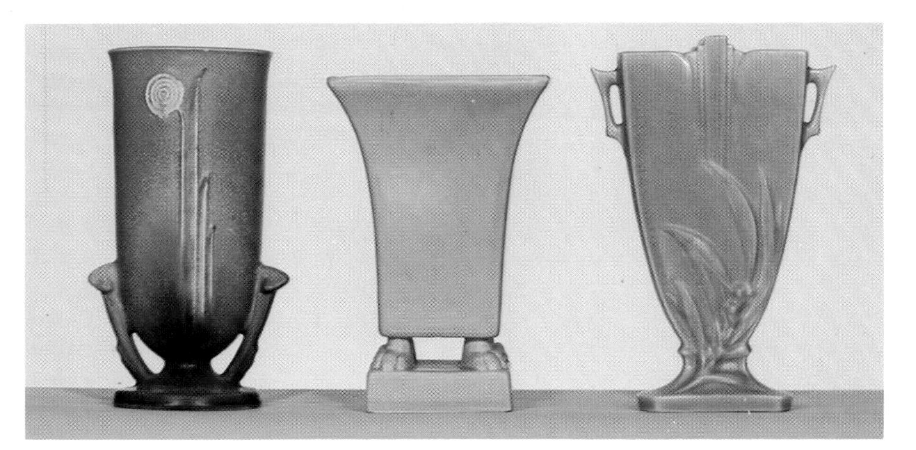
Plate 152

REPRINTS OF ROSEVILLE CATALOGUES

This section contains reproductions of the color plates in the old Roseville catalogues. Some are of seldom seen lines; others are of those lines that are so diversified and dissimilar as to make proper identification difficult.

Although to a large extent, many pages were colored with what appeared to be a thin tint over a black and white photo, in many cases the colors were evidently not quite an accurate indication of actual color. On some pages, only the bisque shapes were shown, unglazed and without any attempt at color. Two of these were Luffa and Russco. Victorian Art Pottery was shown in only white, blank shape outlines. By discovering several pieces, which did not accurately fit in any of the more familiar lines; and in trying to satisfy our curiosity that resulted, we were able to identify them by the shapes and sizes given as Victorian Art Pottery.

Complete lines are not shown, but through comparisons of shapes, handles, glaze texture, etc., these pages may help the collector to identify many of the more unusual pieces.

Autumn, Before 1916

Azurine, Orchid and Turquoise, 1920 (?)

Banks, Early 1900's

Banks, Early 1900's

Blue Tea Pots, Before 1916

Carnelian, II, 1915

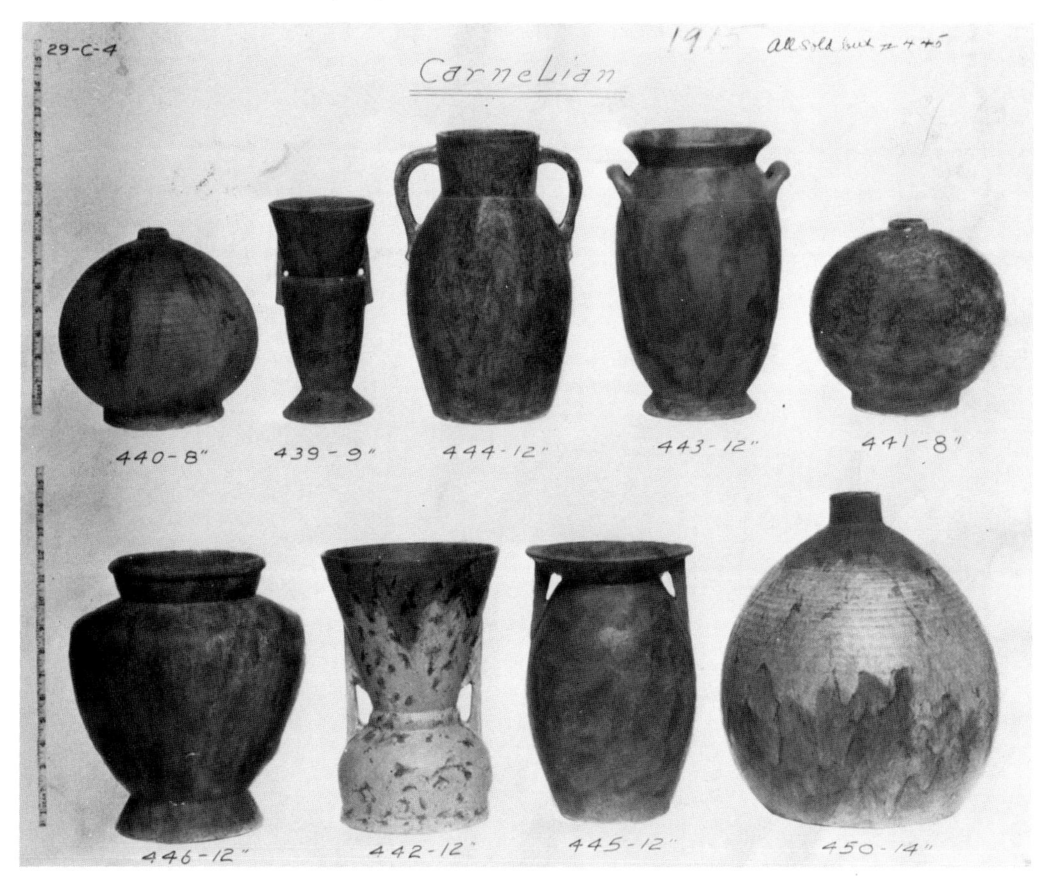

Cameo, 1920

Cameo, 1920

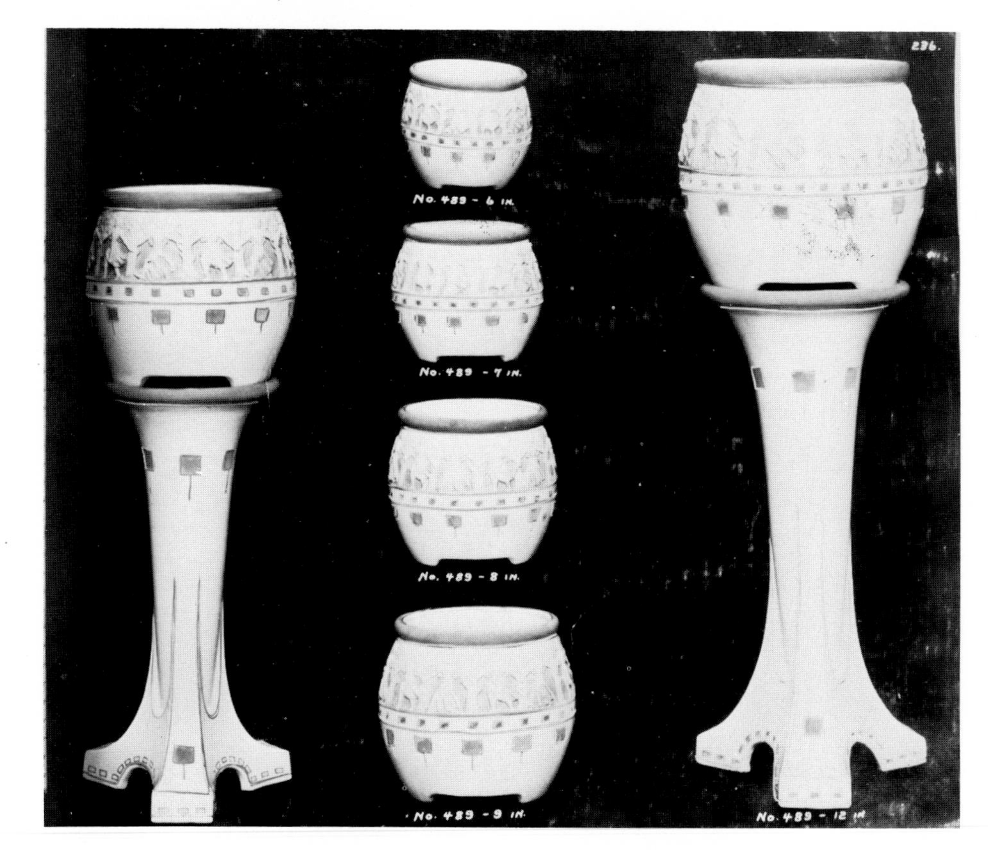

Chloron, 1907

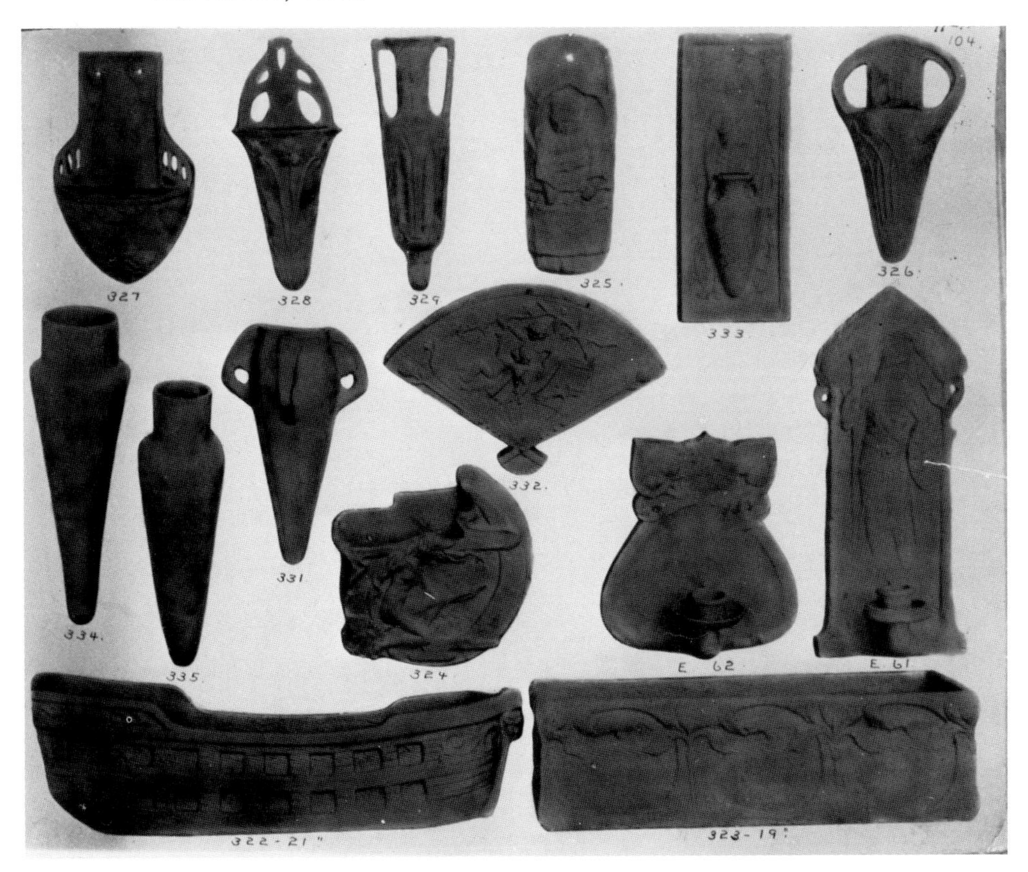

Chloron, 1907

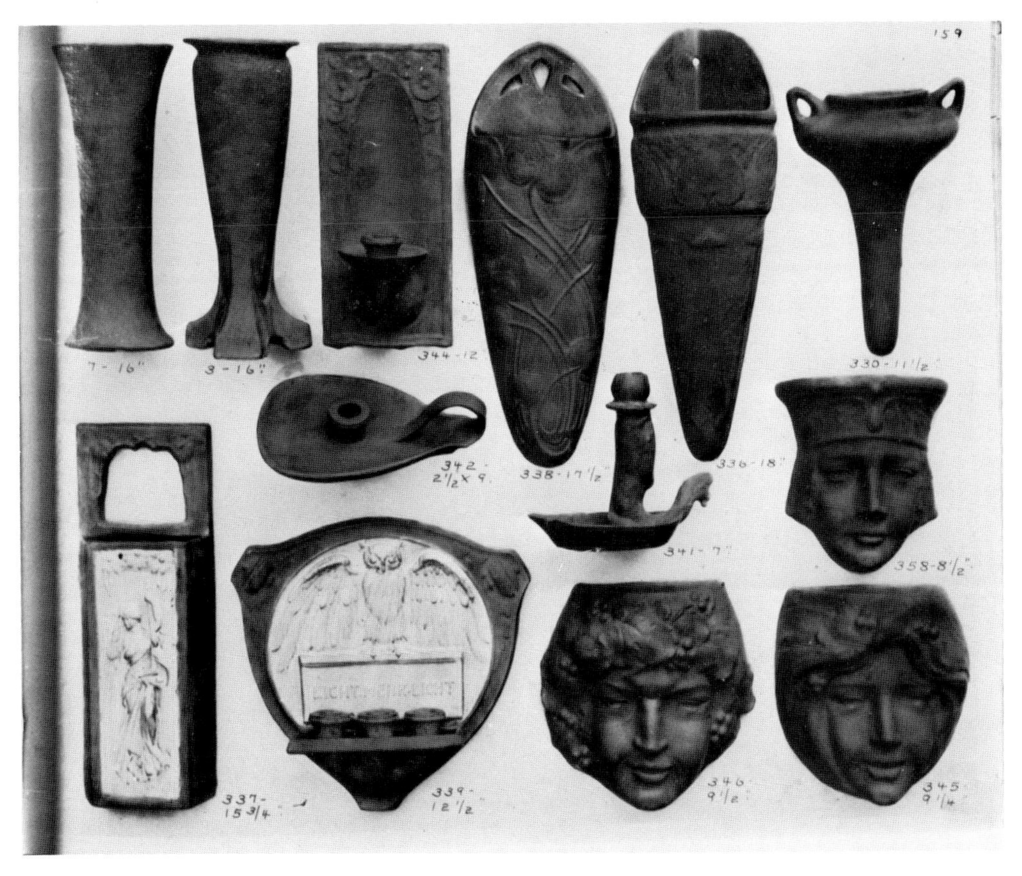

Colonial Toilet Set, 1900's

Cremo, 1916

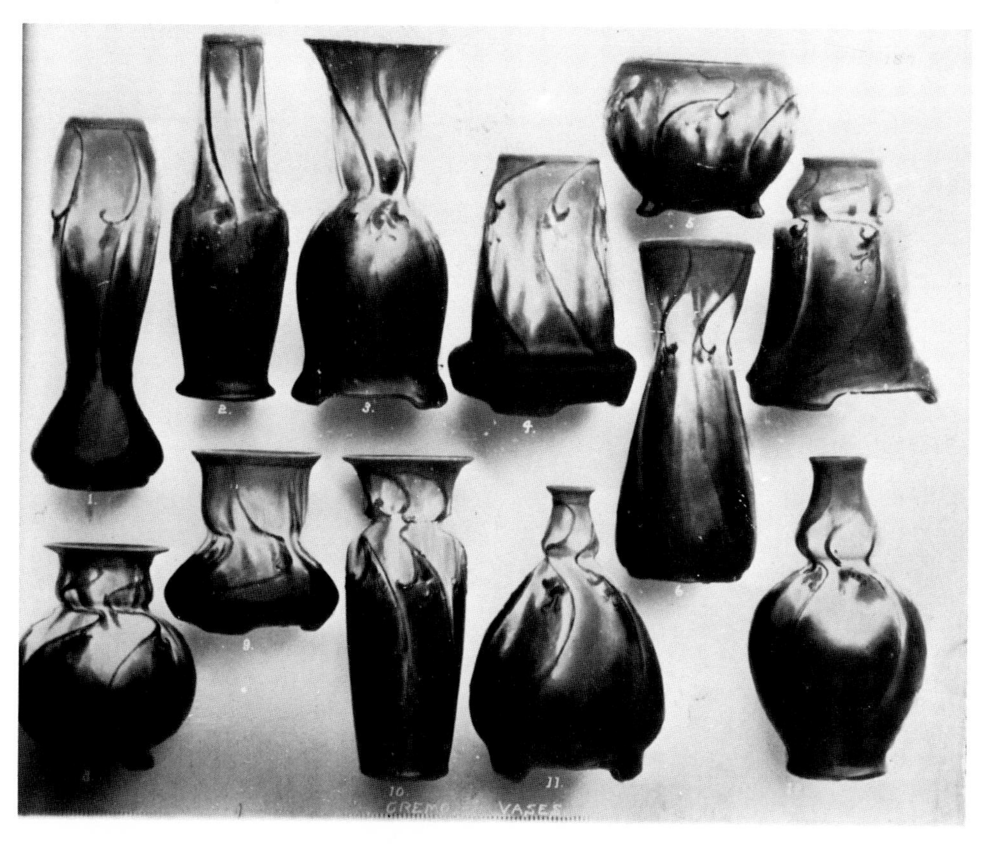

Crystalis (Rozane), 1906

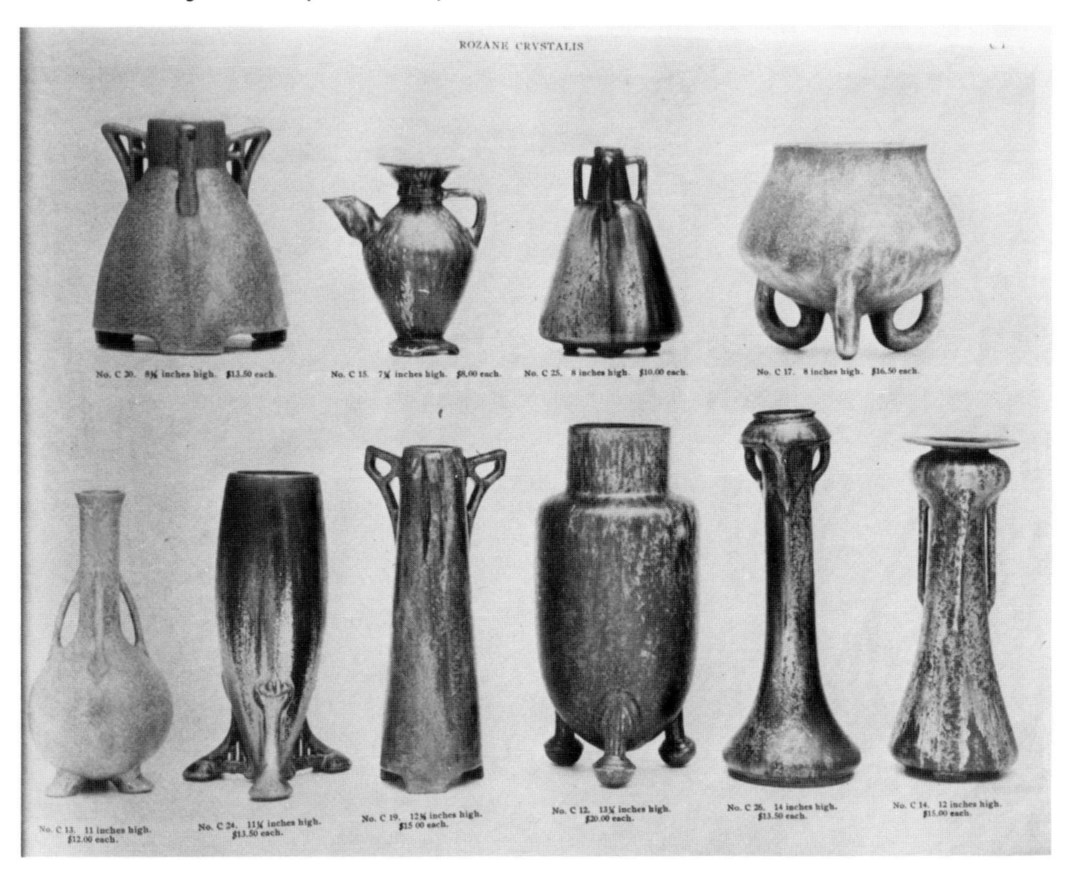

Della Robbia Tea Pots, 1906

Della Robbia (Rozane), 1906

Egypto, (Rozane), 1905

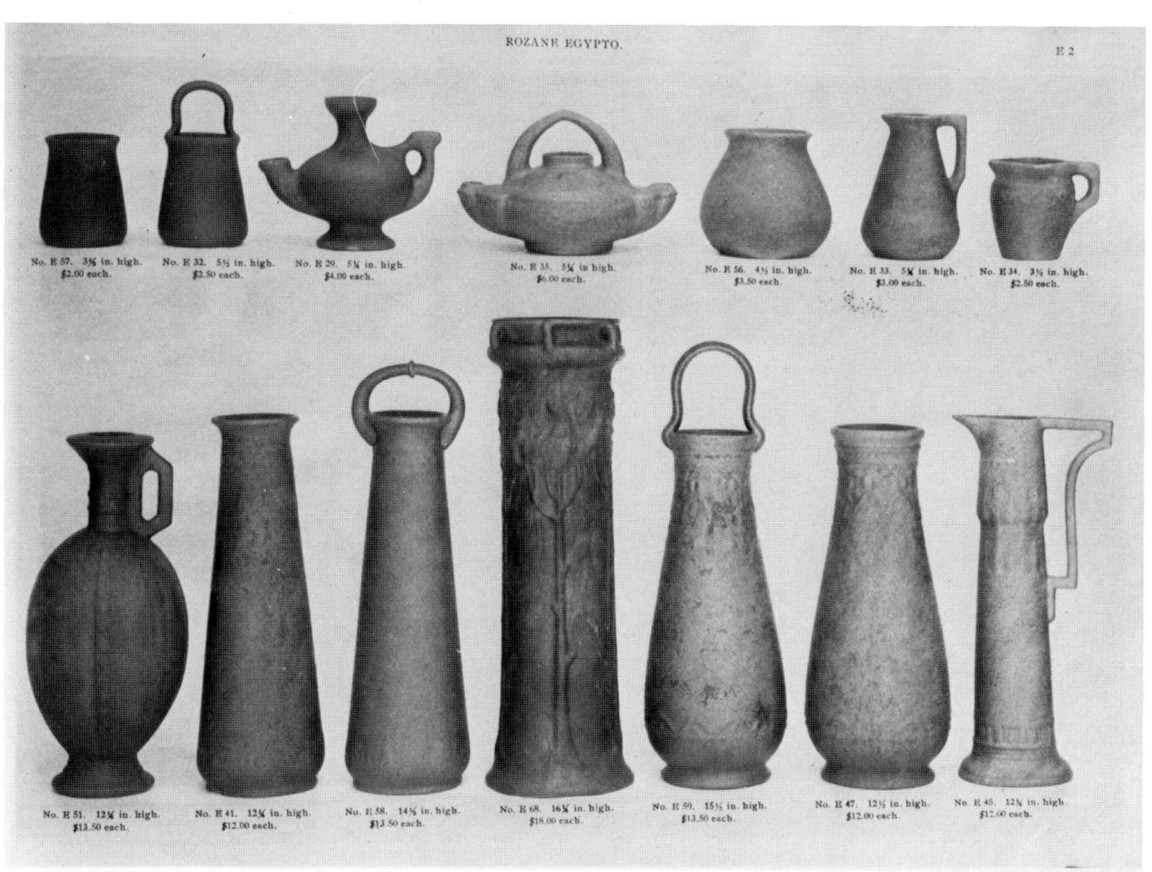

Earlam, 1930

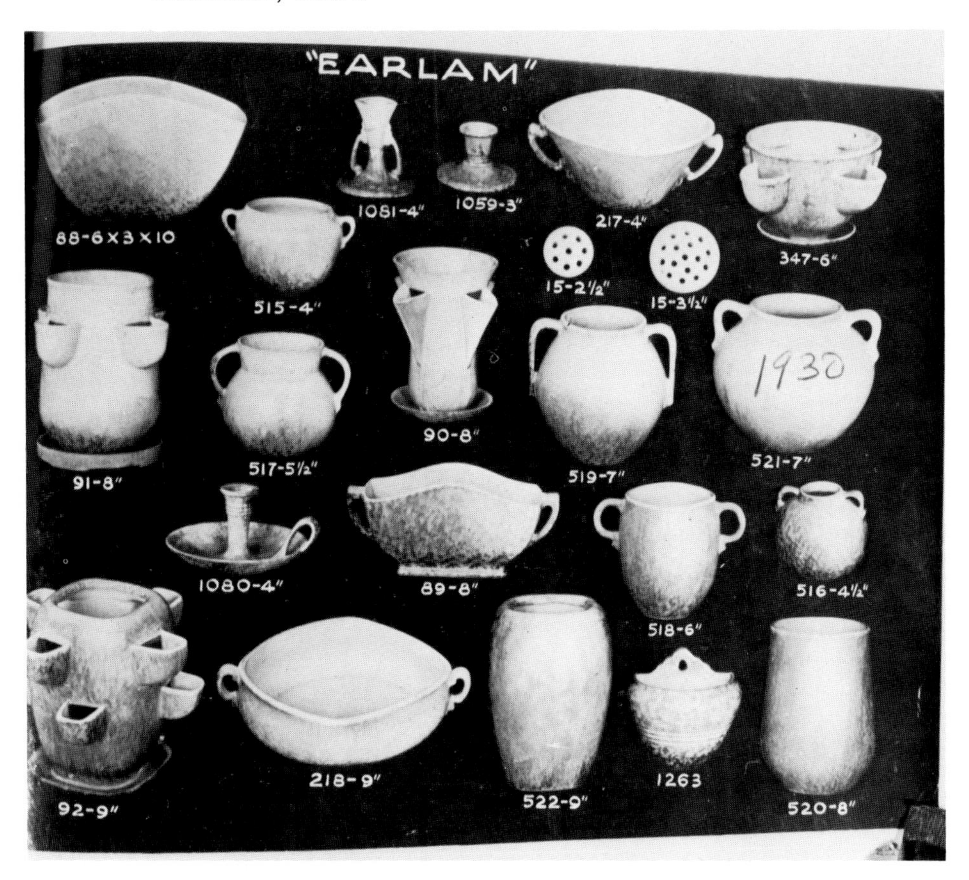

Earlam, 1930

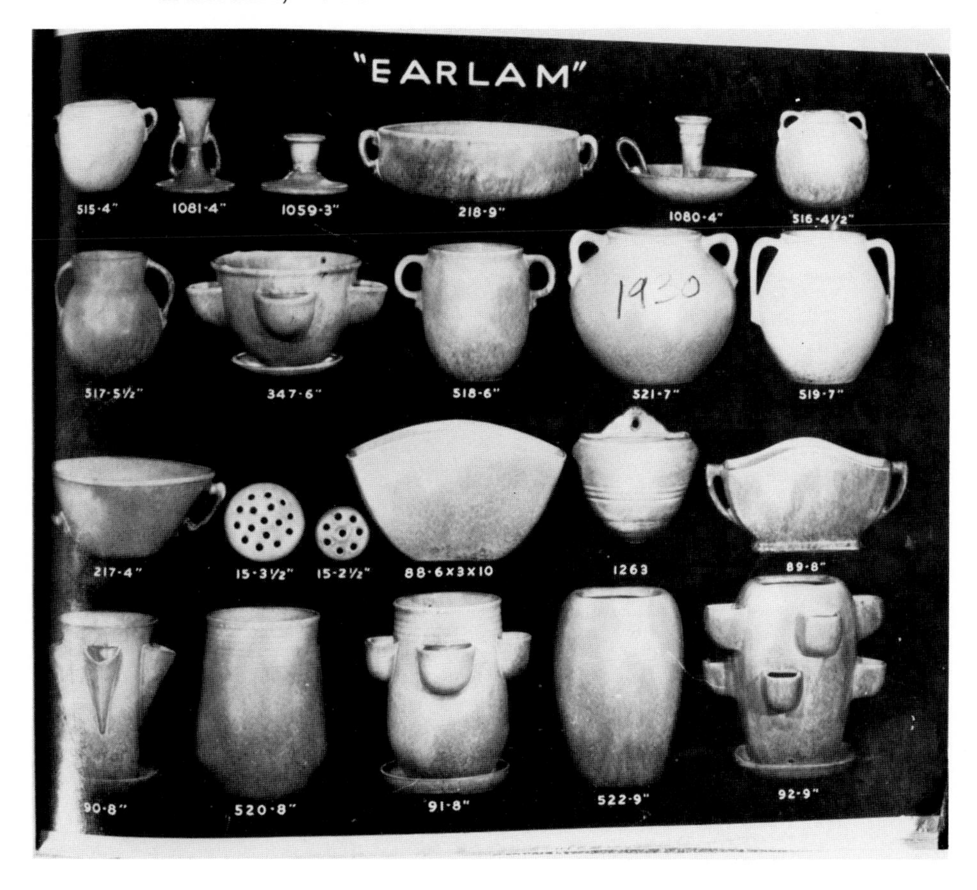

Early Pitchers, Before 1916

Early Pitchers, Before 1916

Futura, 1928

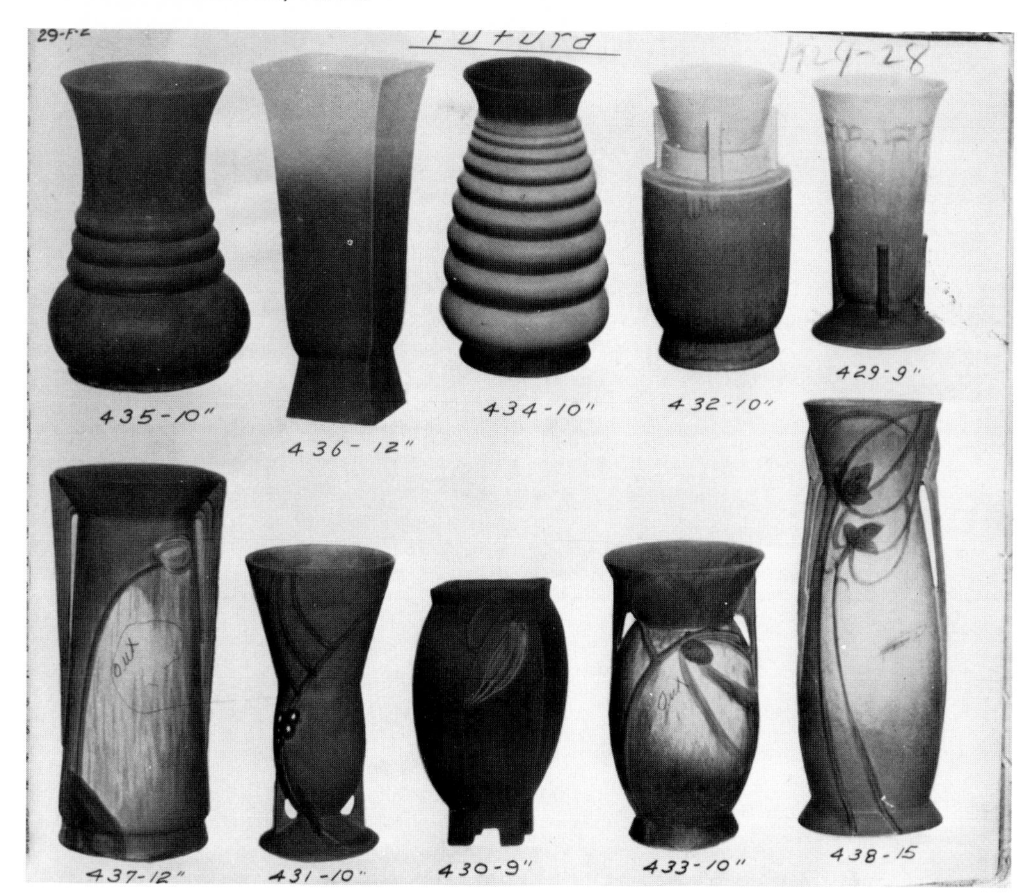

Futura, 1928

Futura, 1928

Futura, 1928

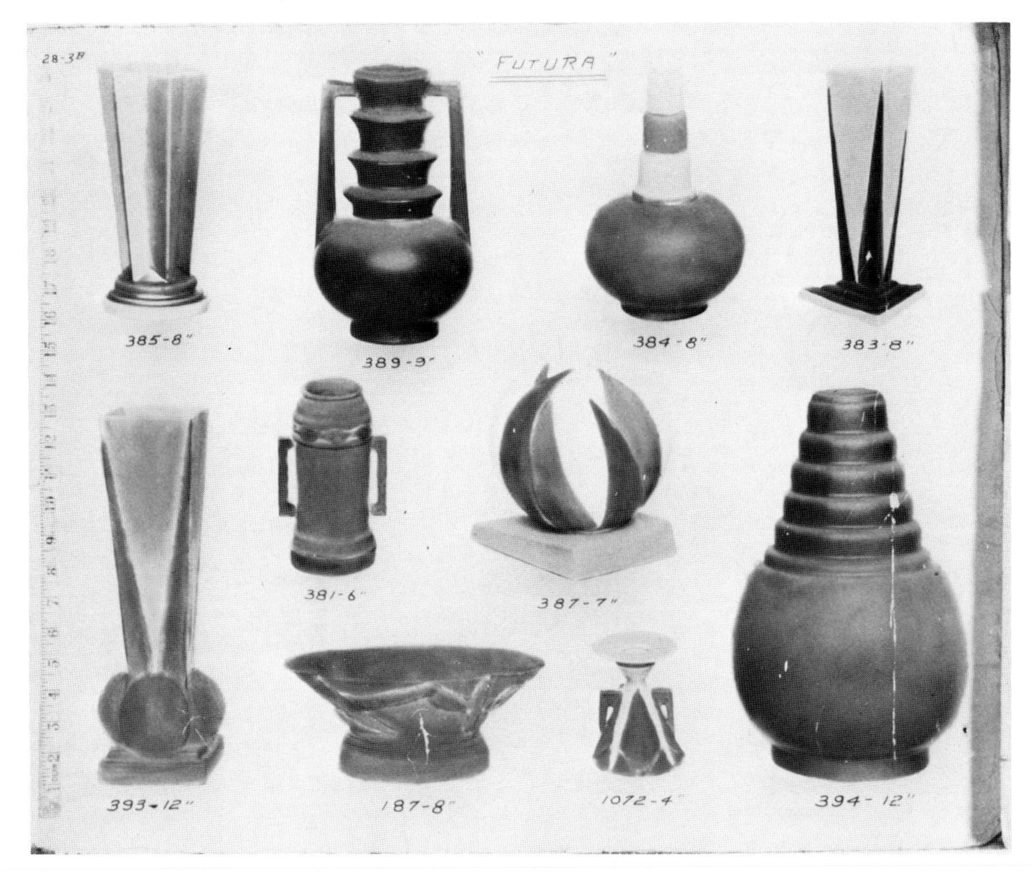

Futura, 1928

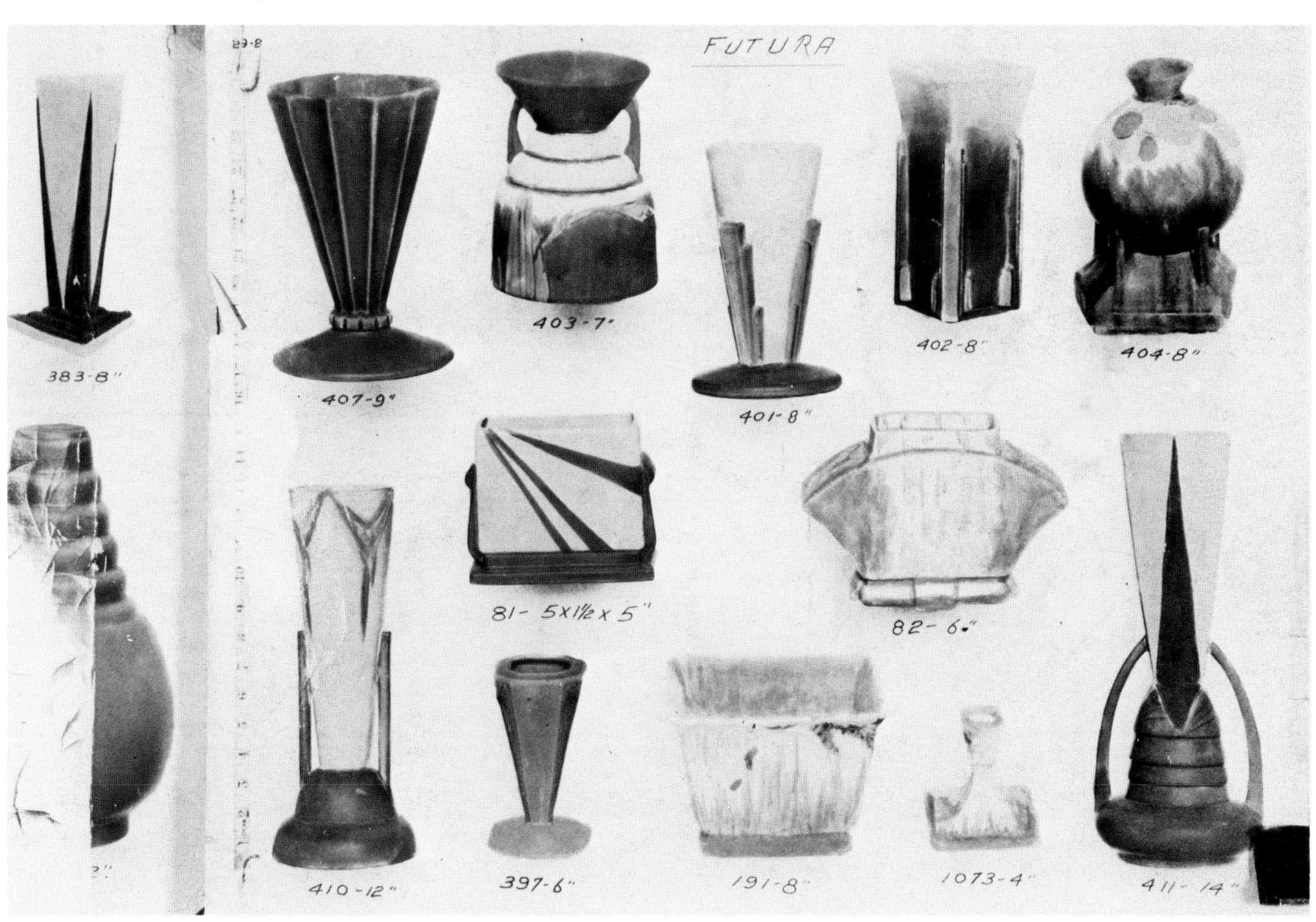
FUTURA
383-8"
407-9"
403-7"
401-8"
402-8"
404-8"
81- 5x1½x5"
82- 6"
410-12"
397-6"
191-8"
1073-4"
411-14"

Garden Pottery, 1931

Gold Traced, Before 1916

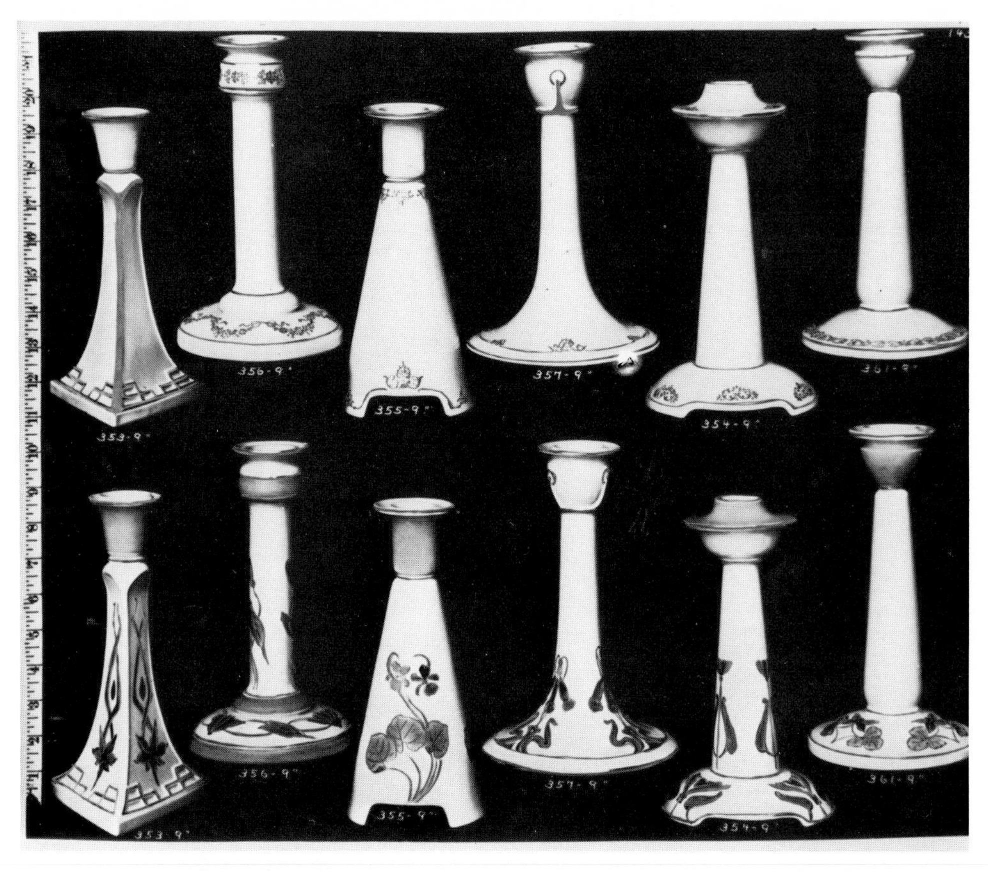

Holland, Before 1916

Individual Tea Sets, Before 1916

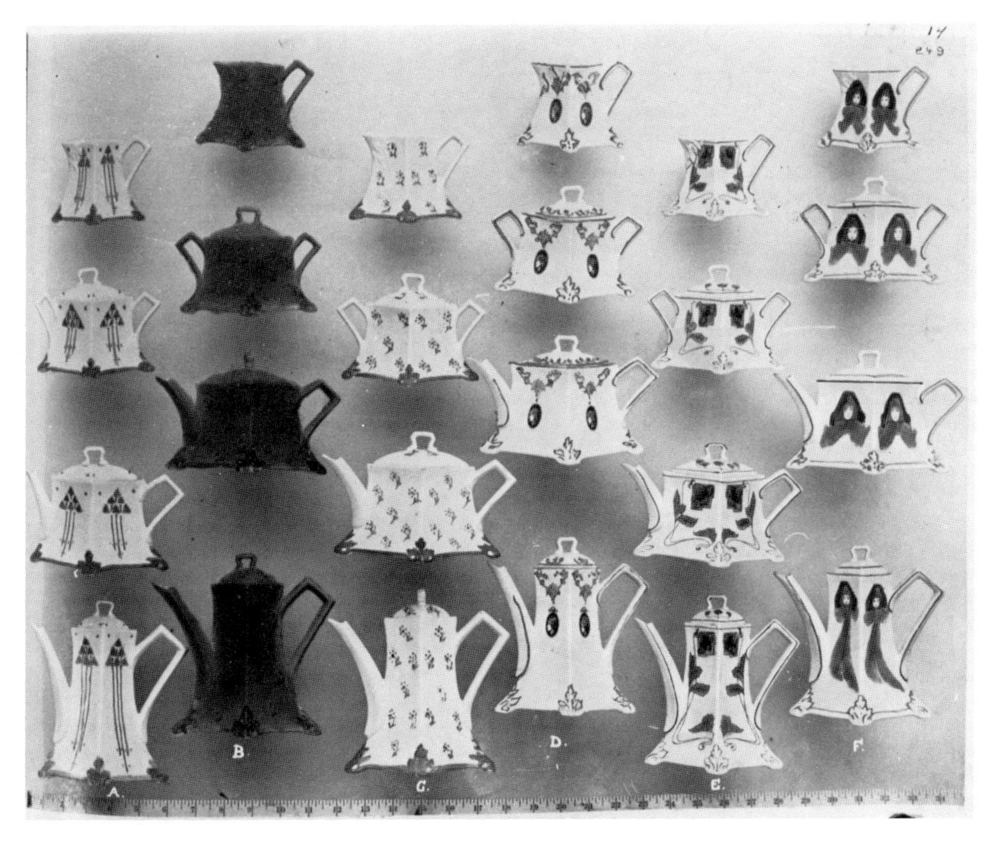

Imperial II, 1924

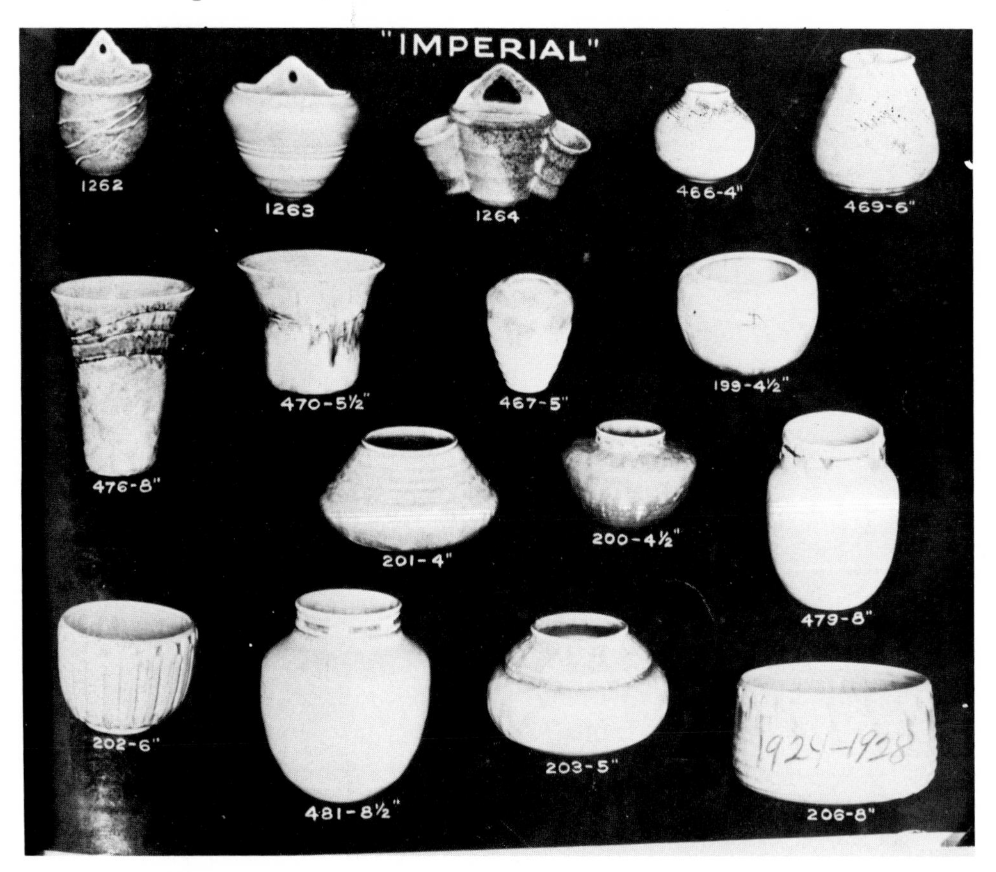

Imperial II, 1924

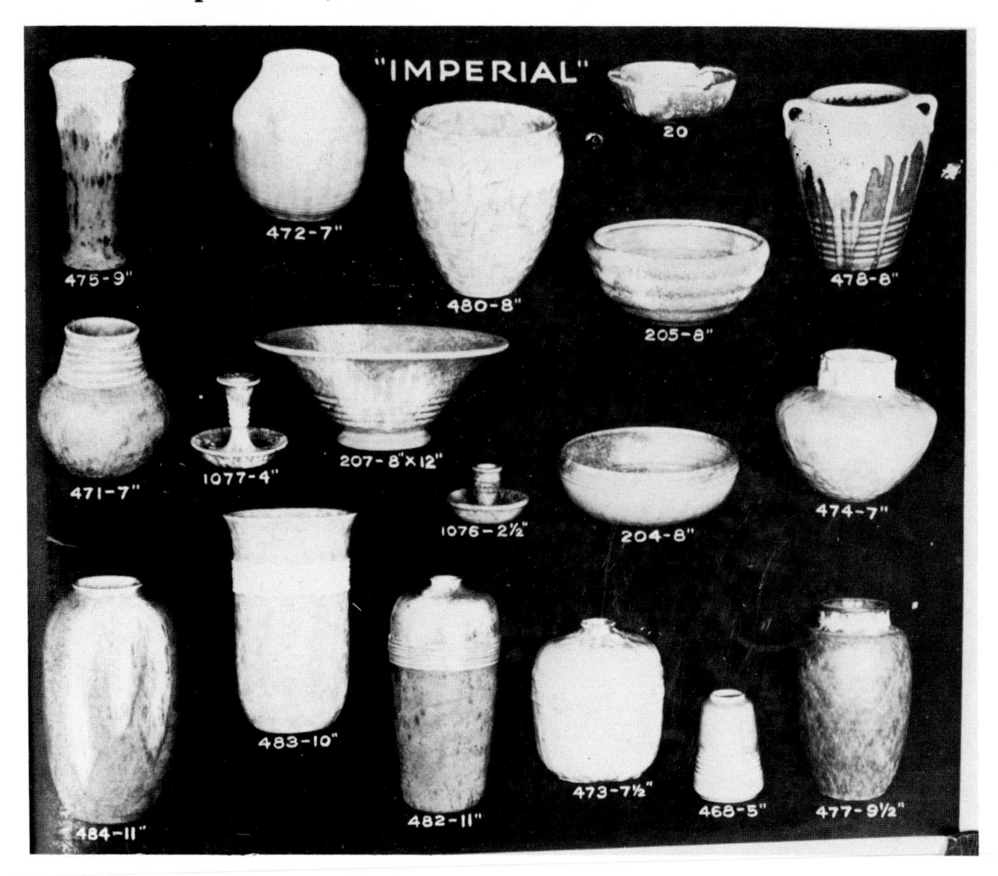

Ivory, Second Line, 1937

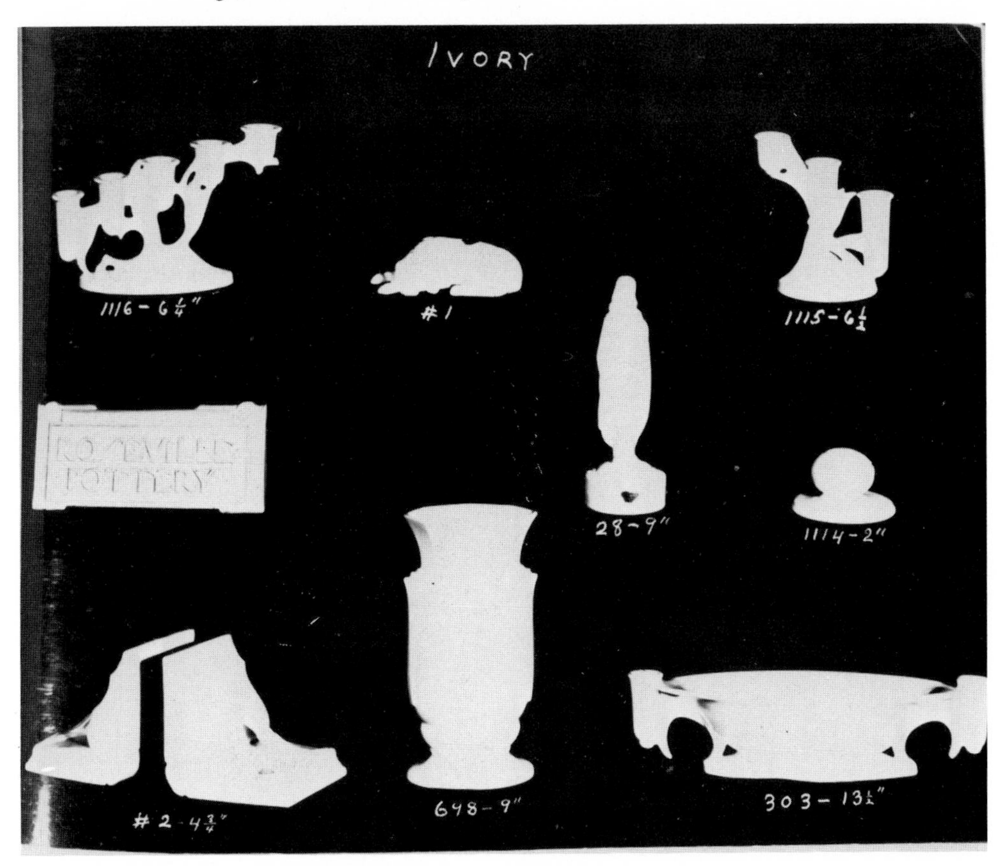

Ivory, Second Line, 1937

Ivory, Second Line, 1937

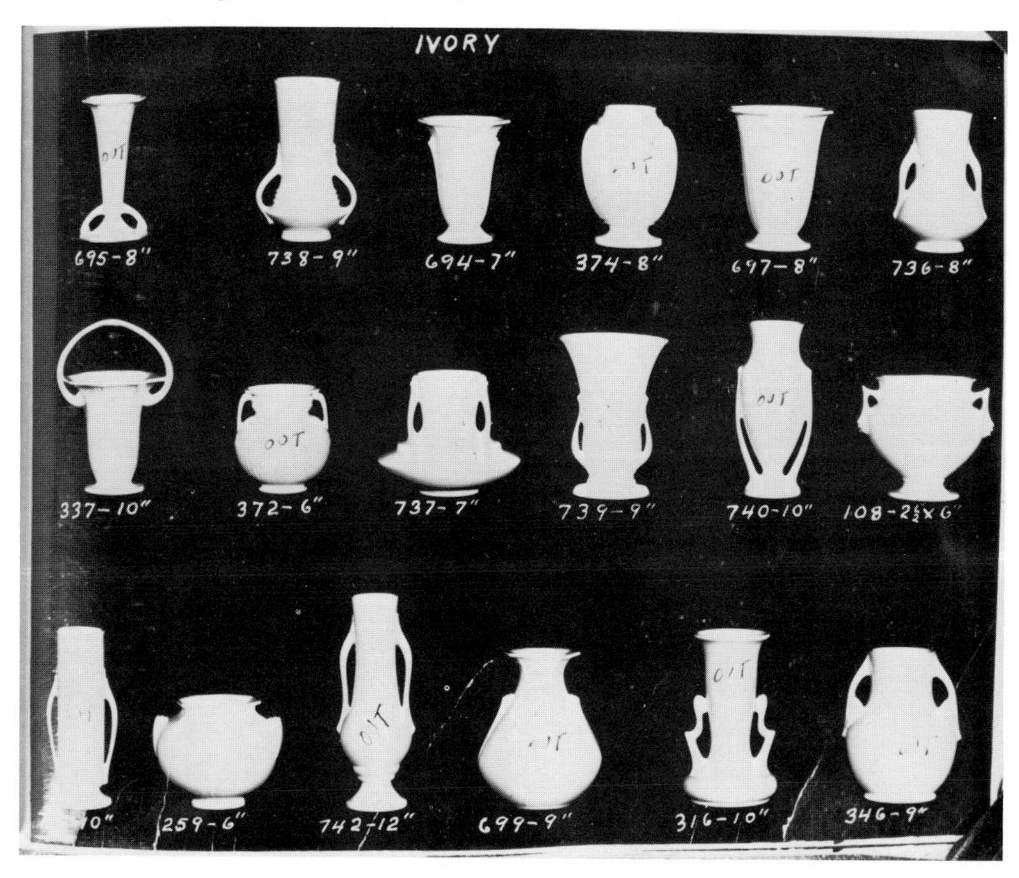

Ivory [Ivory Frieze], and Tints, Before 1916

Juvenile, Before 1916

Juvenile, 1918

Lombardy, 1924

Lombardy, 1924

Lustre, 1921

Lustre, 1921

Jardinieres and Pedestals, Early 1900's

Matt Color, Before 1916

Moderne, 1930's

Novelty Steins, Before 1916

Opac Enamels, 1900

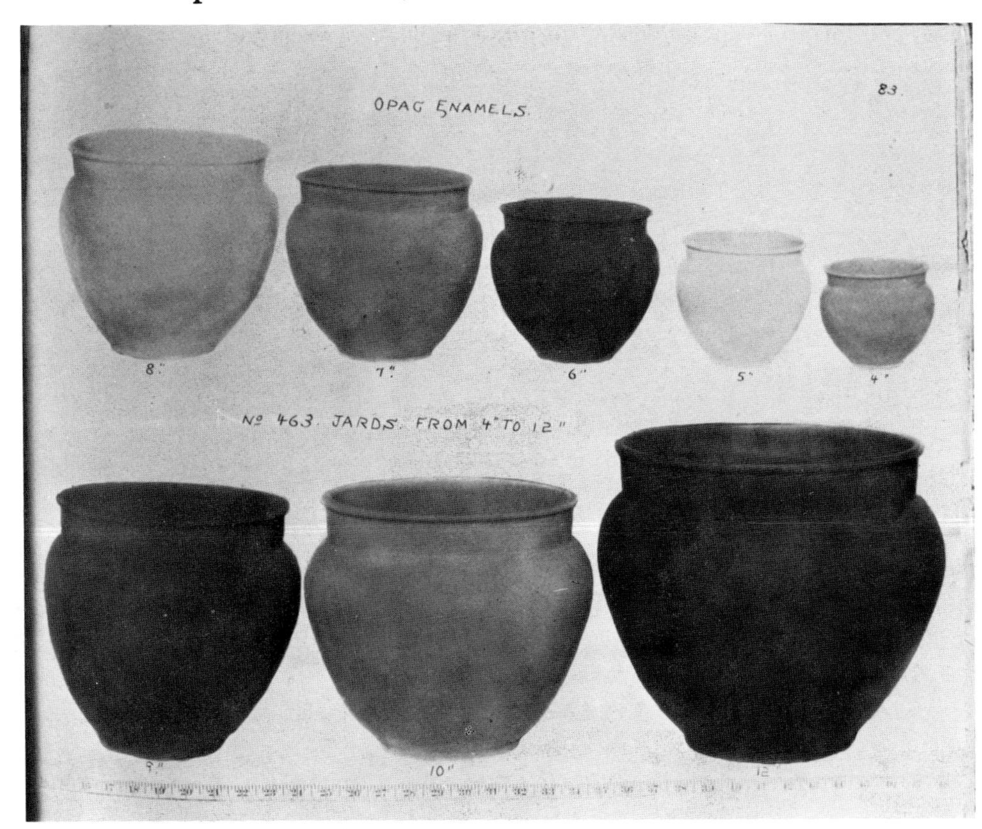

Rozane Pattern, 1940's

Rosecraft, 1916-19

Rosecraft Black, 1916

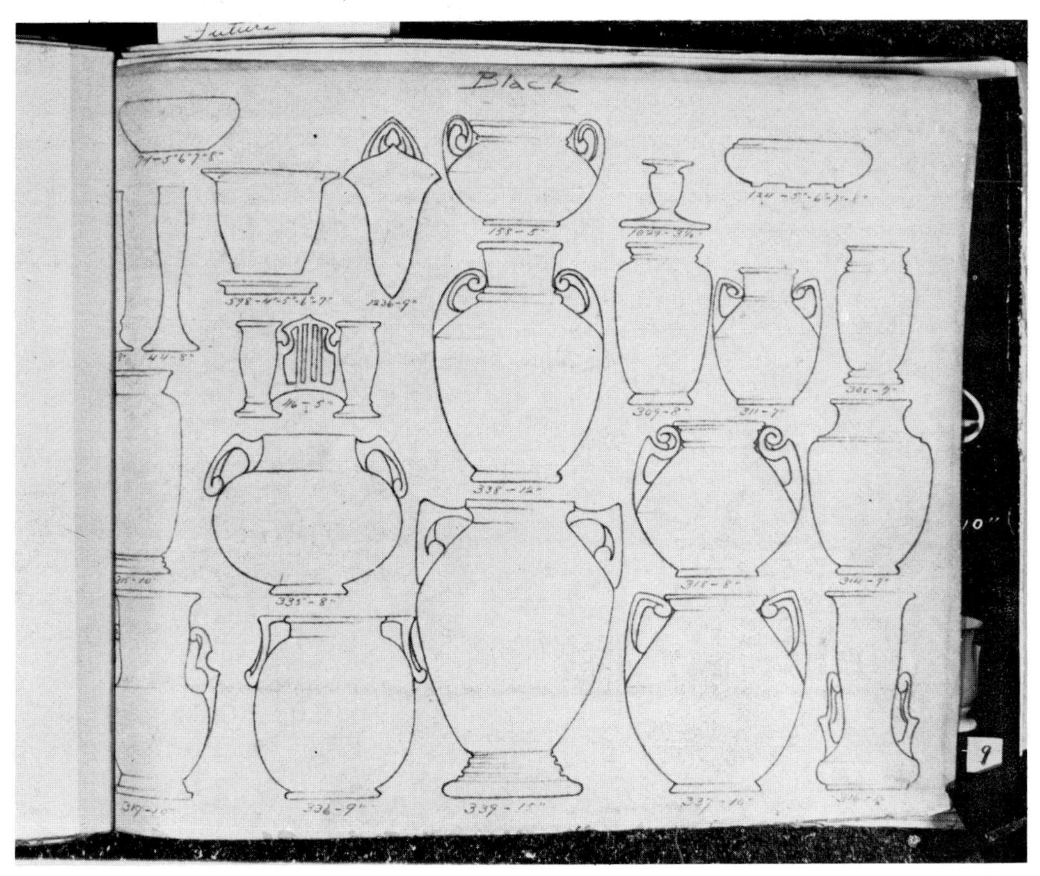

Savona, 1924-28

Sylvan, 1918

Sylvan, 1918

Sylvan, 1918

Tourmaline, 1933

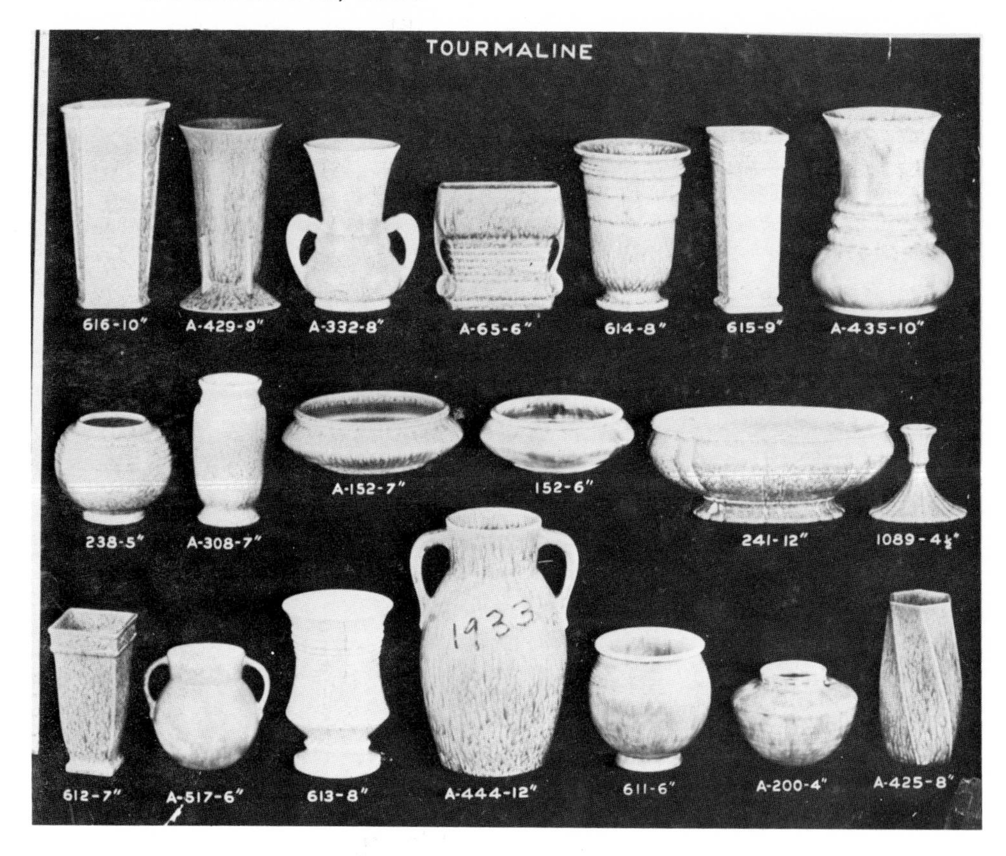

Umbrella Stands, Early 1900's

Victorian Art Pottery, 1924-28

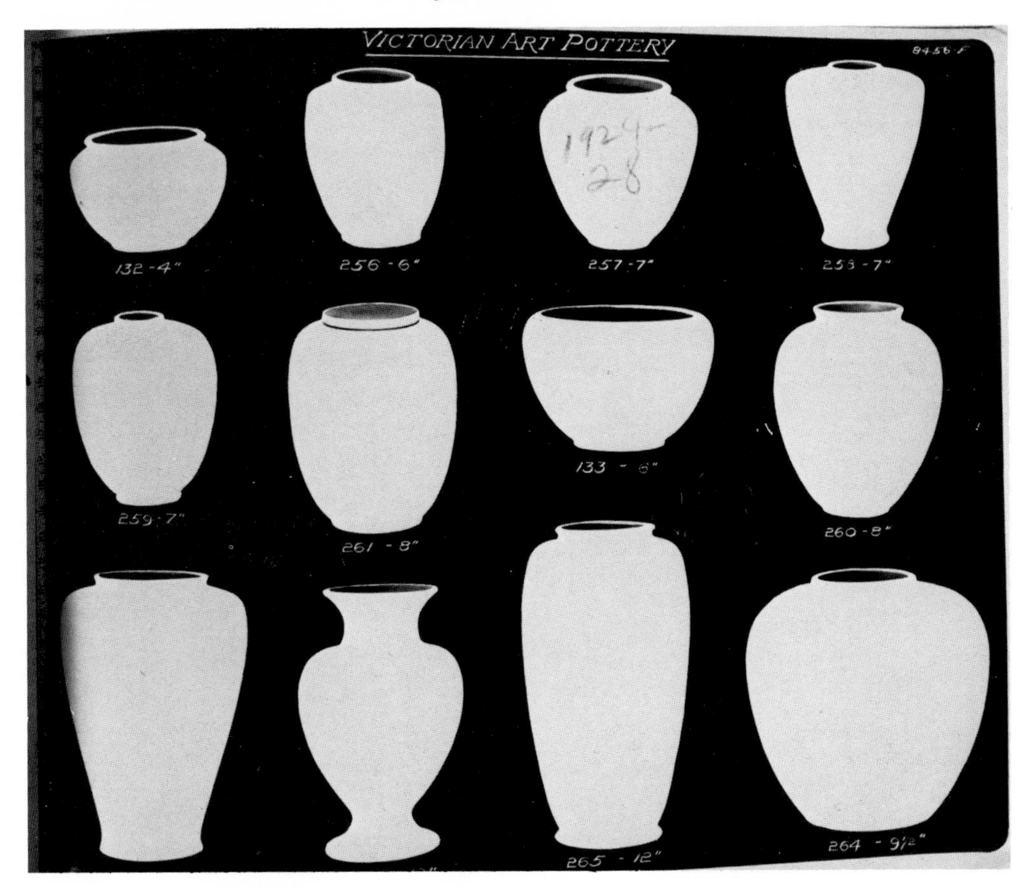

Venetian, Early 1900's.

Shown in composite below, pudding crock and bake pans, Spongeware is Cornelian, early 1900's

Volpato, 1918

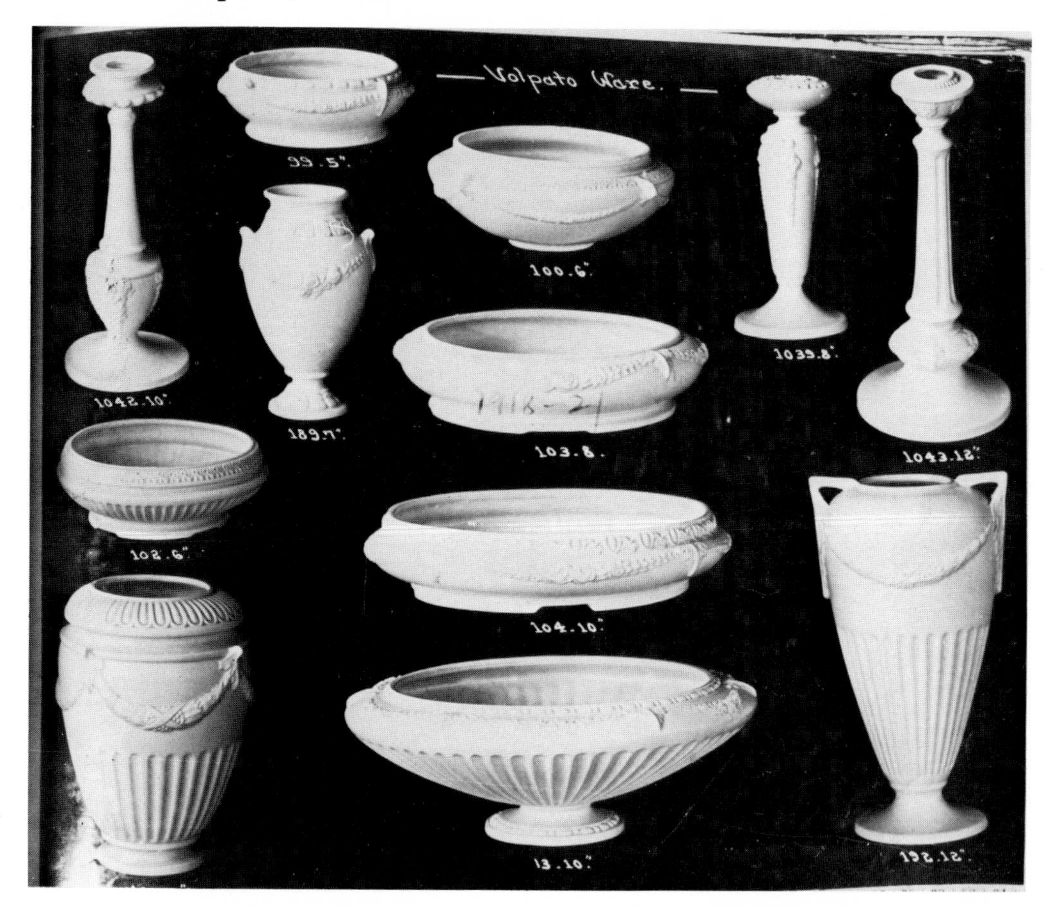

Volpato, 1918

BIBLIOGRAPHY

Alexander, Donald E.; ROSEVILLE POTTERY FOR COLLECTORS; published by the author, 1970.

Buxton, Virginia; private correspondence.

Cobb, Lura Milburn; A VISIT TO SOME ZANESVILLE POTTERIES; The Southwestern Book; December, 1905.

Cox, Warren E.; THE BOOK OF POTTERY AND PORCELAIN; Crown Publishers, 1970.

Evans, Paul; ART POTTERY OF THE UNITED STATES; Crown Publishers, 1975.

Hall, Francis and Gladys; HALL'S PRICING FORMULAS; published by the authors; continually updated.

Henzke, Lucile; AMERICAN ART POTTERY; Thomas Nelson, Inc., 1970.

Kovel, Ralph and Terry; THE KOVELS' COLLECTOR'S GUIDE TO AMERICAN ART POTTERY; Crown Publishers, Inc., 1974.

Muskingum Co. Bibliography, 1905.

Ohio Historical Society; Roseville Records and Daily Ledger.

Peck, Herbert; THE BOOK OF ROOKWOOD POTTERY; Bonanza Books; 1968.

Purviance, Louise and Evan, and Norris F. Schneider; ROSEVILLE ART POTTERY IN COLOR; Wallace-Homestead Book Co., 1970.

Schnieder, Norris; ZANESVILLE ART POTTERY; published by the author, 1963.

GLOSSARY OF RELATED TERMS

Art Pottery — True form of art, unique in shape or decoration, motivated by free expression of one's artistic abilities.

Bisque — Ceramic wares, not yet decorated, having been subjected to only one firing for the purpose of hardening the clay.

Body — Term referring to the particular type and characteristics of the material forming a vessel.

Ceramics — Term used to cover a variety of fired, clay products.

Crazing — The crackled appearance of certain glazes caused by uneven expansion and contraction between body and glaze.

Creamware — Type of highly refined earthenware body, very light in color.

Decalcomania — A picture or design transferred from prepared paper, a decal.

Decorator — One who applies color to a pre-determined design.

Designer — One who developes and sketches proposed shapes, or draws up actual working patterns.

Embossing — Raised design formed on the surface of an item within the mold.

Finisher — One who sponges and smooths out defects in the unfired ware.

Glaze — The glassy finish applied to the decorated surface of pottery as a liquid, and fired in the kiln until it becomes a hard and protective covering for the pottery.

Jigger — Type of molding machine consisting of a paddle or stick which is lowered into the mold, pressing the clay into the sides of the mold while it is spinning on the wheel.

Lustre — A glaze with the platina of metals, produced through the use of metallic oxides.

Molds — Sectional forms which are used to shape pottery, either by casting, in which case liquid clay or slip is poured into the mold, allowed to stand until desired thickness adheres to the wall of the mold, the excess then poured out; or by jiggering.

Muffle Kiln — Oven used to permanently affix decoration or color on pottery, operates at a relatively low temperature.

Overglaze — Method of decorating over the glaze, and refiring at a low temperature causing the decoration to become permanent.

Porcelain — A mixture, containing a high content of silica is soft fired, leaving a porous body, which readily apsorbs the glaze and becomes translucent in the refining; china.

Pottery — Earthenware, contains less silica than porcelain, and when fired becomes so dense as will not absorb the glaze; the body remains opaque.

Pouncing — Method in which waxed patterns, perforated so as to allow powdered talc to sift through to the surface of the ware, thus transfers the out lines of the design, which is then completed by the decorators.

Sagger — Boxes in which unfired ware was placed, used to protect the pottery as it was fired in the kiln.

Sang de Beouf — Literal meaning, ox blood; copper glaze resulting in a true red color.

Second — Any item not meeting standard quality control as first grade, but not having serious imperfections.

Sgraffito — Method of decoration where the pattern is incised into an outer layer of clay, thereby exposing a second layer of color.

Slip — Mixture of clay and water, used for casting in the molds; colored and used for painting; or in a heavier consistency, forced through a device which made threads of clay used to decorate the surface of the pottery.

Slip Ware — Pottery decorated by the squeeze bag technique, wherein slender threads of soft, colored clay are piped on over an already existing background color.

Underglaze Decoration — Method of decorating pottery, using the colored slip previous to the glazing process.

ALPHABETICAL INDEX OF ROSEVILLE PATTERNS

Numbers in parenthesis indicate color plates, catalogue reprints are noted within brackets.